Jan,

Enjoy the desserts!

Lisa Jobs

Sensational Stevia Desserts

❧ ✳ ❧

By

Lisa Jobs

**DISTRIBUTED
BY
NUTRI-BOOKS**

Copyright ©2005 by Lisa Jobs
Healthy Lifestyle Publishing LLC
P.O. Box 80311
Valley Forge, PA 19484
610-265-7102 phone & fax

This book utilizes stevia extract in the recipes. Stevia can be used as an alternative to sugar and artificial sweeteners. The FDA has approved stevia as a dietary supplement. Before using stevia or any sugar alternative, consult with your physician. The information in this book has not been evaluated or approved by the FDA. The products and recipes mentioned herein are not intended to diagnose, treat, cure or prevent any disease and do not constitute medical advice of any kind.

Although the recipes, information and recommendations in this book are presented in good faith and believed to be correct, neither the author nor the publisher make any representations or warranties as to the completeness or accuracy of the information or in the health benefits, or lack thereof, of stevia or any other product mentioned herein. The information in this book is supplied upon the condition that the persons receiving the same will make their own determination, in consultation with their physician, as to its suitability for their purposes prior to use.

In no event will the author or the publisher be held responsible for damages of any nature whatsoever resulting from the use of or reliance upon the information in this book or the products to which the information refers. Neither the author nor the publisher warrants the accuracy or timeliness of the information in this book and shall have no liability for any errors or omissions in the information. Except as specifically stated, neither the author nor the publisher make any endorsements of any products mentioned herein.

Publisher's Cataloging-in-Publication
(Provided by Quality Books, Inc.)

Jobs, Lisa.
    Sensational stevia desserts / by Lisa Jobs.
    p. cm.
    Includes bibliographical references and index.
    LCCN 2005923639
    ISBN 0-9765245-4-6

    1. Desserts. 2. Cookery (Stevia)
    3. Low-carbohydrate diet—Recipes.   I. Title.

TX773.J63 2005   641.8'6
                        QBI05-200097

Photography by Charles George Jobs
Food Styling by Lisa Jobs
Clip art by Charles George Jobs
Edited by Gina Colau
Cover and Interior design by Bookcovers.com
Printed in Korea

Front Cover Photo: Wonderful White Chocolate Chip-Cranberry Cookies, pg. 12; Italian Cannoli, pg. 58; Classic Coconut Macaroons, pg. 14.

Table of Contents

Dessert Recipes
I. Cakes•Icings

II. Cookies

III. Pies•Tarts

IV. Squares•Bars

V. Crepes•Cobblers•Dumplings

VI. Puddings•Mousses•Custards

VII. Specialty Desserts

Acknowledgements

I'd like to thank the following important people who helped me in the huge task of completing this book:

My husband Chuck for his encouragement, support, patience and invaluable work on the clip art, cover, insert and author photos. What can I say, you are wonderful!

My sons, Christian and Alex, for their countless taste testing of my recipes.

Mary Toboulidis for all of her help in the kitchen preparing these recipes. You have been a pleasure to work with, and a devoted and trusted friend. I'm so thankful to have been blessed with knowing you. Let's not forget, you've been like a third grandmother to Christian and Alex!

My parents, in-laws, family members and friends, especially Rose Perri, who tried the recipes, rated them and provided great feedback. I really appreciate it!

My mom who helped me appreciate homemade desserts as I was growing up... from her incredibly tasty pizzelles at Christmas time and popular Italian sponge cake for birthdays to the warm cinnamon sugar donuts after school. Thanks for all of your hard work and love that went into your homemade desserts.

Foreword

Defeat Diabetes Foundation, Inc. is a 501 (c)(3) nonprofit organization dedicated to improving the lives of all diabetics. Defeat Diabetes Foundation is also committed to preventing diabetes from occurring in the first place. This is an awesome responsibility, which we take very seriously. And I, as an insulin-dependent diabetic and Executive Director of Defeat Diabetes Foundation, am constantly searching for ways to accomplish these goals. Our motto is:

AWARENESS + ACTION = PREVENTION®

For this reason Defeat Diabetes Foundation is proud to endorse Sensational Stevia Desserts. It provides awareness to the general public of a wonderful and natural alternative to desserts containing high amounts of sugar.

When I first learned of the opportunity to write the foreword for Sensational Stevia Desserts, I needed more information on the benefits of incorporating stevia into my diet. As an insulin-dependent diabetic, I am always looking for ways to reduce my sugar intake and still enjoy the foods I want to eat. After doing much research, and with Lisa's help, I realized that there really is a viable natural alternative available. I hope our endorsement of Sensational Stevia Desserts will open your eyes to this natural alternative to sugar and how you can make it part of your diet.

The conversion table at the beginning of the book and the caloric comparisons to traditionally prepared desserts make it easy for everyone to see the benefits offered in these recipes.*

*Please note that an acceptable substitute for low fat or nonfat milk is Lactaid® or soy milk. Also, please consult with your medical/nutrition team to determine your individual restriction, if any.

As an added benefit, I am pleased that Healthy Lifestyle Publishing LLC, publisher for Sensational Stevia Desserts, is making a donation to support our Defeat Diabetes® Awareness Programs.

For more information: www.DefeatDiabetes.org

A. P. Mandell

Andrew P. Mandell
Executive Director
Defeat Diabetes Foundation, Inc.

Introduction

Finally, a stevia cookbook that specializes only in desserts you crave and nothing else! From classic chocolate layer cake to the most decadent truffles, you'll be impressed with how delicious they taste...all with no aspartame, saccharin, sucralose or sugar added, just all-natural stevia extract!* **Sensational Stevia Desserts** helps make stevia dessert options plentiful. The book's focus is also on lowering carbohydrates and substantially reducing sugar content of tasty desserts—without sacrificing flavor!

This is the first and only stevia cookbook to offer you the stevia conversions for three different stevia brands! This helps you determine the exact stevia amount necessary for a wonderfully tasting, sweet dessert the first or second time you make it! Keep in mind that these are great guidelines but your taste preferences may vary.

I hope you'll also appreciate the nutrition facts per serving that are included with each recipe. Having the nutritional data allows you to analyze your particular dietary needs. Whether it's to watch your calories, count your carbohydrates and sugar grams or reduce your sodium, it's all there for you!

Other fascinating and interesting aspects of the book are the comparisons that I made with some of the stevia recipes and their comparable sugar recipe or store-bought counterparts. Many of the nutritional facts for these recipes are nothing short of amazing and truly eye-opening! You may not want to use sugar again in your dessert recipes!

Another goal of the book is to make it easier and more convenient for you to incorporate stevia into your dessert recipes without requiring ingredients that are hard to find. Most ingredients are readily available in your local supermarket—only a few are more obscure items. So, for your convenience, I include specific resources on where to purchase them, and some include approximate costs.

After most of the recipes, you'll find my personal comments and ideas, like how the recipe differs nutritionally from products at the grocery store or how the choice in ingredients can make such a difference in health value and nutrition. I've also included variations to many of the recipes so that you can change one or two ingredients and have a new recipe to try!

While it's true that stevia desserts typically taste a little different from their sugar counterparts, many of these recipes come so, so close to the real thing! I'm confident that if you gave some of the pie recipes to your coworkers or friends to try without telling them that you used stevia, they wouldn't be able to tell the difference. Take, for instance, my favorites... Keeper Key Lime-White Chocolate-Cheese Pie, Positively (Divine) Peanut Butter Pie and the Sinfully Cinnamon Cream Cheese Pie... all I can say is Yum!

My final note is a sincere "Thank You" to Andy Mandell, Executive Director, Defeat Diabetes Foundation for writing the foreword to **Sensational Stevia Desserts**. I wish you much success as Defeat Diabetes® awareness programs continue to enhance the lives of diabetics around the world.

I feel so blessed to have the opportunity to present this stevia dessert cookbook to you! I sincerely hope that this helps you make better dessert choices for your and your family's health! Have fun and explore the many possibilities.

Lisa Jobs

Some sugar may be inherent in ingredients like chocolate chips.

Brief Overview of Stevia and Its Advantages

Many of you may already be familiar with all that stevia offers you, but for those who aren't, here's a summary for your perusal. If you want more information on stevia—its uses, its origin and more—you can search online under the keyword "stevia" for a significant amount of data.

*Stevia is 200-400 times sweeter than sugar, therefore very little is needed as a replacement for sugar. The typical conversion is one teaspoon of stevia to one cup of sugar, however, this will vary depending on the stevia manufacturer or brand.

*Stevia is an all-natural alternative to the artificially made, chemical sweeteners available on the market today. There are no known side effects, unlike other substitutes.

*Stevia rebaudiana extract is derived from an herbal plant and is grown in many different parts of the world including China, Thailand, Paraguay and Brazil.

*Stevia has been used extensively as a sweetener in Japan since the 1970s. Product applications have ranged from diet soda to soy sauce.

*Stevia is heat-stable, so you can successfully bake with it, unlike some artificial sweeteners like saccharin and aspartame.

*Stevia has no calories, carbohydrates, fat, sugar, aspartame, saccharin or sucralose.

Stevia does not affect blood glucose levels so it may be of interest to diabetics.

*The FDA has approved stevia as a dietary supplement.

*Good sources of information on stevia studies and research include these two Web sites: www.steviacanada.com and www.raysahelian.com.

*Check with your physician before using stevia to be sure it is recommended for your particular dietary needs.

Important Tips to Know
Before Making a Recipe

1. The recipes are only as good as the ingredients you use. This applies particularly to the stevia you purchase. Be sure to use only the highest quality, best tasting stevia extract you can find. Even the other ingredients I chose to use in the recipes were among the finest, so try to take advantage of high-quality ingredients when possible for the most delicious end product you've ever tasted.

2. The sweetness *potency* of stevia brands varies, so you must account for this in your baking. You may need to adjust the stevia measurements listed in these recipes based on the particular brand you use. See next page for stevia measurement conversions.

3. Your sweetness *preference* also dictates how much stevia you may want in a recipe, so use my measurements as a guideline. You may have to adjust the stevia amount to reflect your personal preference.

4. Be sure ingredients are at room temperature unless otherwise noted.

5. Be patient and try each recipe at least *two* or even *three* times due to the variances listed in #2 and #3. It will be worth it, just *don't give up after only one try!*

6. Microwave oven wattage varies, so when I list the time to heat something in a recipe, note that this is based on an 850 watt microwave oven. You may have to adjust based on where you live and if your oven wattage is higher or lower.

7. When mixing ingredients like butter and eggs for cookies and cakes, keep in mind that the mixture will not "cream" as it will when using sugar in traditional dessert recipes. However, it will incorporate when the dry ingredients are added.

8. Stevia will not brown or caramelize like sugar, so in traditional recipes where this is important, stevia may not be an appropriate substitute.

9. Bake in the center rack of the oven unless otherwise stated.

Stevia Measurement Conversions

Many stevia manufacturers and other health-related companies offer a variety of stevia products. It can be confusing and even frustrating to determine the exact amounts of stevia to incorporate into a recipe since the sweetness potency varies greatly by manufacturer. The two types of stevia used in this book include the pure powdered extract and, in only two cases, the convenient stevia packets. For your convenience, I've compiled an easy-to-use stevia measurement conversion table for three stevia brands.

The "generic" stevia extract listed on each recipe was my former company's brand, Sweetvia® pure stevia extract. Our product was fairly potent compared to most brands, so you need the least amount of it when baking. Use Sweetvia® stevia brand measurements when using a fairly strong stevia extract. The other two brands, Sweet Leaf® and Astraya®, are similar in quality and taste to Sweetvia® stevia but not quite as potent, so they were used for comparison. Use these amounts as guidelines in each recipe. Your sweetness preference may vary.

Stevia extract (Sweetvia®)	Sweet Leaf®	Astraya®
1 pinch	⅛ tsp.	⅛ tsp.
⅛ tsp.	¼ tsp.	¼ tsp.
¼ tsp.	½ tsp.	½ tsp.
⅓ tsp.	½ tsp.	½ tsp.
½ tsp.	¾ tsp.	¾ tsp.
⅜ tsp.	¾ tsp.	¾ tsp.
¾ tsp.	1 ¼ tsp.	1 ⅛ tsp.
¾ tsp.- (for Pumpkin Custard)	1 ⅛ tsp.	1 tsp.
1 tsp.	1 ½ tsp.	1 ¼ tsp.
1 ¼ tsp.	1 ½ tsp.	1 ½ tsp.
1 ¼ tsp. - (for Lemon-Poppy Seed Cookies)	1 ¾ tsp.	1 ¾ tsp.
1 ½ tsp.	2 tsp.	2 tsp.
1 ¾ tsp.	2 ¼ tsp.	2 ⅛ tsp.
2 tsp.- (for Almond Pound Cake)	2 ¾ tsp.	2 ½ tsp.
2 tsp.- (for No-Bake Mint Chocolate Cheesecake)	2 ½ tsp.	2 ¼ tsp.
2 ¼ tsp.	2 ¾ tsp.	2 ¾ tsp.
2 ½ tsp.	3 tsp.	2 ¾ tsp.
3 ¾ tsp.	4 ¼ tsp.	4 tsp.

Nutritional Facts Source

I am so pleased that Wendy Hess, Registered Dietician and Certified Diabetes Educator, provided the nutritional facts for this cookbook. As a Vermont-based nutrition professional with over 20 years of experience, she uses several state-of-the-art databases to analyze the nutrient profile of recipes and food products for chefs, Web sites, food writers, cookbook authors, and food producers. She primarily employs Nutritionist Pro (First Data Bank) software to analyze the recipes in this book. For information, call 1-802-863-3033 or contact her via e-mail at wendyhess@adelphia.net.

For the most part, the nutritional profiles are for primary recipes only. However, in some instances profiles for variations are provided. Also, optional ingredients are not included in the recipe analyses.

Abbreviations and Codes Used in This Book

Carbohydrates- Carbs
Grams- g
Ounce- oz.
Pint- pt.
Package- pkg.

Packages- pkgs.
Refrigerator- fridge
Tablespoon- Tbsp.
Teaspoon- tsp.

Stevia Sources

A wide range of stevia products and sources are available as of this writing. Use the following sampling as a guideline for your convenience.

Astraya® Stevia: Astraya, 1-403-828-6292, www.astraya.com or e-mail josh@astraya.com.

NuNaturals® White Stevia: NuNaturals, Inc., 1-888-753-4372, www.nunaturals.com or e-mail info@nunaturals.com.

Stevia powder, liquid and spoonable stevia: Stevia Canada/ Global Stevia Corp., www.steviacanada.com or e-mail office@steviacanada.com.

Sweetleaf® Stevia: SweetLeaf, 1-800-899-9908, www.buywisdom.com or e-mail wisdom@wisdomnaturalbrands.com.

Lisa's Favorite Cakes/Icings

*Almond Pound Cake with Chocolate Icing

*Lemon Pound Cake with Raspberry Sauce

I've always been partial to pound cake over layer cake so choosing the type of cake was easy. However, both of the pound cakes are so moist and luscious that it's hard to pick my favorite. Try both and see which one you like better!

Suggestions When Baking Cakes:

1. *I prefer to use sea salt and unbleached flour in my recipes because of their additional health benefits and less refined nature. However, they do tend to cost more. You can substitute them for table salt and all-purpose bleached flour if you wish.*

2. *Make sure ingredients are at room temperature! Unless otherwise noted, soften butter for few hours before mixing it in a recipe.*

3. *If you don't have time to soften the butter, take it out of the fridge, cut it in small pieces and heat it in a microwave-safe dish for 15 seconds on power level 5 or medium power.*

4. *Pre-measure all ingredients prior to mixing so that you reduce the possibility of overmixing.*

5. *Place baking pans on rack in the center of the oven.*

6. *Use unsalted butter because you can include the exact amount of salt you want in a recipe without the extra sodium you may not need in the salted butter.*

7. *When mixing the butter with the eggs and stevia, be aware that the mixture will not "cream" as it does in traditional sugar recipes, rather the butter will still be separate from the eggs. The mixture will incorporate when the dry ingredients are added.*

Almond Pound Cake

Serving Size: 1 slice • **Total Servings:** 12

Make sure ingredients are at room temperature. Pre–measure all ingredients prior to mixing so you reduce possibility of overmixing.

2 cups unbleached flour
¼ tsp. sea salt
½ tsp. baking soda
1 tsp. baking powder

⅓ cup unsweetened, natural applesauce
½ cup (1 stick) unsalted butter, softened
3 large eggs
1 large egg white
2 tsp. stevia extract (see page xii for brand variances)
¼ cup + 2 Tbsp. instant nonfat dry milk
½ cup plain low-fat (or nonfat) yogurt
½ tsp. almond extract

Preheat oven to 350° F. Spray a loaf cake pan with canola oil spray. Remove excess spray by wiping pan with paper towel and then flour pan. Sift flour, salt, baking soda and baking powder. Measure applesauce and place in strainer with bowl underneath. Let juice drain out of applesauce for a few minutes. Set aside or discard juice and keep drained applesauce.

Beat butter with electric mixer until blended well. Beat in eggs and egg white one at a time. (The mixture will not "cream" as it does in traditional sugar recipes, rather the butter will be separate from the eggs. However, it will incorporate when dry ingredients are added.) Add stevia and dry milk to egg mixture. Scrape sides of bowl to assure thorough mixing. Heat yogurt in microwave for 15 seconds. Mix in yogurt, applesauce and almond. Remove about half of liquid mixture from mixing bowl and set aside.

Divide dry ingredients into thirds in a large bowl. Place first third of dry ingredients in another bowl. With electric mixer on medium-high speed, mix first third of dry ingredients with half of liquid ingredients. Scrape sides of bowl for better incorporation. Mix in second third of dry ingredients and scrape sides of bowl again. Add the remaining half of liquid ingredients. Mix for about 30 seconds. Then, add last third of flour mixture to the bowl and mix for about 30 seconds. Scrape sides of bowl again. Be sure not to overmix.

Pour batter into pan and smoothen top of batter with a knife. Bake in bottom oven rack for 20 minutes. After 20 minutes, place a cookie sheet on top rack to protect top of cake from getting too dark. Bake another 25 to 30 minutes or until toothpick inserted in the center comes out clean.

Cool cake before removing from pan. Frost with desired icing (see pages 8-10) or cut in small pieces and dip in carob or chocolate fondue (see page 61) or fruit fondue (see page 64) .

Sugar Comparison

Nutrition Facts/Serving
-1 slice

	This Recipe	Traditional "Sugar" Recipe
Calories	183	570- Over 2.5 times more!
Carbohydrates	19g	74g- Almost 3.5 times more!
Total Sugars	3g	50g- Almost 17 times more!
Fiber	less than 1g	less than 1g
Fat	10g	28g-Almost 3 times more!
Cholesterol	75mg	133mg
Sodium	144mg	204mg
Protein	5g	7g

What a *substantial* difference in calories, carbs, sugar and fat!

Variation: Lemon Pound Cake

Prepare above recipe, but omit almond extract and replace with 1 Tbsp. lemon extract. For variety, try drizzling raspberry sauce (see page 49) on the cake or dipping it in your favorite fruit fondue (see page 64) .

Lisa's Note: This cake has a crusty top that is atypical of most pound cakes, but it sure is scrumptious nonetheless!

Chocolate Layer Cake

Serving Size: 1 slice • **Total Servings:** 12

Make sure ingredients are at room temperature. Pre-measure all ingredients prior to mixing so you reduce possibility of overmixing.

1 ¾ cups + 2 Tbsp. unbleached flour
½ cup + 1 Tbsp. cocoa powder
¼ tsp. sea salt
1 tsp. baking soda
¾ tsp. baking powder

½ cup (1 stick) unsalted butter, softened
3 large eggs
2 large egg whites
3 ¾ tsp. stevia extract (see page xii for brand variances)
½ cup instant nonfat dry milk
½ cup nonfat plain yogurt
¼ cup water
⅓ cup unsweetened applesauce
1 tsp. vanilla extract

Preheat oven to 350° F. Spray with canola oil spray and flour two 8" layer cake pans. Remove excess spray by wiping pans with paper towels. Sift flour, cocoa powder, salt, baking soda and baking powder. Mix sifted ingredients and set aside. Beat butter with electric mixer. Quickly beat in eggs and egg whites one at a time. Add stevia. (The mixture will not "cream" as it does in traditional sugar recipes, rather the butter will still be separate from the eggs. But it will incorporate when dry ingredients are added.) Scrape bottom and sides of mixing bowl periodically to assure thorough mixing. Add dry milk to butter/eggs and continue mixing. Heat yogurt for 15 seconds. Mix in yogurt, water, applesauce and vanilla to butter/eggs mixture for only about 1 to 2 minutes. Remove about half of liquid mixture from mixing bowl and set aside.

Divide sifted ingredients into thirds in a large bowl. Place first third in a separate bowl. With electric mixer on medium-high speed, mix first third of dry ingredients with half of liquid ingredients for 30 seconds. Scrape sides of bowl for better incorporation. Mix in another third of sifted ingredients and scrape sides of bowl again. Mix for about 30 seconds. Add the remaining half of liquid ingredients and mix for 30 seconds. Then, add last third of flour mixture and mix for about 30 seconds. Scrape sides of bowl again. Be sure not to overmix.

Pour batter into pans and smoothen top of cakes with a knife. Bake for 35 to 40 minutes or until toothpick inserted in center comes out clean. Let cakes cool in pans before removing. Run knife around edges of cake pans to help loosen cakes. Frost with desired icing (see pages 8-10) .

Sugar Comparison

	Nutrition Facts/Serving -1 slice

	This Recipe	**A Leading Chocolate Cake Mix**
Calories	202	270- 25%more!
Carbohydrates	23g	35g- 1.5 times more!
Total Sugars	3g	21g- 7 times more!
Fiber	2g	1g
Fat	10g	13g
Cholesterol	75mg	55mg
Sodium	213mg	350mg
Protein	7g	3g

With these nutritional specs, you won't mind giving your kids these cupcakes...or splurge for yourself!

Variation: Chocolate Cupcakes

Serving Size: 1 cupcake, Total Servings: 17

Spray cupcake pans with canola oil spray. If you prefer to use paper cups in the pan, be sure to spray them since the batter may stick to the paper. Then pour batter into cupcake pans (or paper cups) and bake for 18 to 20 minutes or until toothpick inserted in center comes out clean. Yields 17 cupcakes. I know it's an odd number, but I like the size of the cupcakes this way. Of course, you can add less if you want to squeeze 18 out of the recipe.

Nutrition Facts/Serving	
Calories	143
Carbohydrates	16g
Total Sugars	2g
Fiber	2g
Fat	7g
Cholesterol	53mg
Sodium	150mg
Protein	5g

Lisa's Note: *As much as I would love to recommend freezing this cake for later use, I don't suggest it. I have tried freezing it and although it's still good when thawed, it's not as moist as before freezing. Bottom line—enjoy it as soon as possible after you make it. Store it in a plastic cake container or on a plate with plastic wrap over it at room temperature until ready to serve. Serve within two days. Ice the cake shortly before serving. After icing the cake, be sure to store it in the fridge due to the cream cheese in the icing recipe.*

If this cake cracks a little when baking, don't fret, it will be fine. Once it's removed from the oven and has cooled, the cracks will come together nicely, and you'll be ready to frost a delicious cake. Remember that stevia, combined with these other ingredients, does not react the same way as sugar in baking, so we must account for that sometimes. The good news is that you will not sacrifice taste, quality or compliments when you, your family and your friends have it for dessert.

This recipe was by far the most challenging, as well as the most gratifying. I have never seen or tasted such a delicious stevia recipe for a traditional chocolate layer cake with no sugar, just stevia! I believe that you and your children will love it! I put it to the test of my kids and they kept asking for more. Just think of how much less sugar your children will ingest when substituting this recipe for mixes or traditional chocolate cake recipes.

No-Bake Mint Chocolate Cheesecake

Serving Size: 1 slice • **Total Servings:** 16

4 oz. unsweetened baking chocolate
2 tsp. stevia extract (see page xii for brand variances)
1 tsp. peppermint extract
4 (8 oz.) pkgs. Neufchâtel cream cheese, very soft
2 cups water
1 ½ envelopes unflavored gelatin
prepared cheesecake crust (see recipe on page 23)

Nutrition Facts/Serving	
Calories	185
Carbohydrates	4g
Total Sugars	2g
Fiber	1g
Fat	17g
Cholesterol	43mg
Sodium	229mg
Protein	7g

Melt chocolate in microwave for one minute on power 5 or medium heat level. Stir and heat again for another minute on power 5 or medium heat level. Be careful not to burn. Add stevia and peppermint extracts. Mix well. Combine cream cheese and chocolate mixture using electric mixer. In the meantime, boil water. After water is boiled, quickly add gelatin and stir until dissolved. Add to cream cheese mixture and mix well on very low speed. Cover spring form pan with homemade crust.* Place filling into spring form pan. Chill for 2 to 3 hours until firm.

*Optional: If you don't have time to make your own crust, breakup a prepared piecrust and press firmly down on the bottom of a spring form pan.

Chocolate Cheesecake Bites

Serving Size: 1 mini-muffin cake bite • **Total Servings:** 22

8 oz. (½ pt.) heavy cream
2 tsp. vanilla extract
½ tsp. stevia extract, divided (or 12 stevia packets)
    (see page xii for brand variances)
8 oz. pkg. Neufchâtel cream cheese
¼ cup unsweetened cocoa powder

Nutrition Facts/Serving	
Calories	68
Carbohydrates	1g
Total Sugars	0g
Fiber	0g
Fat	7g
Cholesterol	23mg
Sodium	45mg
Protein	1g

Prior to making recipe, lay cream cheese out at room temperature for about 1 to 2 hours. Freeze mixing bowl and beaters for 5 minutes. (This maintains volume so cream doesn't thin out.) Sift cocoa powder.

In a deep bowl, whip heavy cream until *soft* peaks form. Add vanilla and ¼ tsp. stevia extract (or 5 stevia packets) and whip until *stiff* peaks form. In a separate mixing bowl, mix cream cheese until soft using 2 to 3 Tbsp. of the whipping cream mixture to thin the cream cheese. Once the cream cheese is smooth, add the cocoa and the other ¼ tsp. stevia extract (or remaining stevia packets), mixing well. The chocolate cream cheese mixture will be thick. Place mixer on high speed and add chocolate cream cheese mixture to the whipped cream. Scrape sides of bowl for thorough blending of ingredients and mix.

Place small paper cups in mini muffin pan and spray with canola oil spray. Drop in cheesecake bite mixture by the tablespoonfuls. Cover and place in the freezer at least 1 hour before serving. Remove from freezer for about 5 minutes before serving.

Lisa's Note: *I found this recipe on the Internet. It was originally developed by Vicki Speece and reprinted with her permission. These cheesecake bites are so good; I was thrilled to be able to include them in this book.*

Cream Cheese Icing

Makes enough to spread on the pumpkin bars on pages 39.

½ tsp. stevia extract (see page xii for brand variances)
3 Tbsp. 2% milk
1 ½ pkg. (12 oz.) Neufchâtel cream cheese,* softened

Nutrition Facts/Serving	
(2 Tbsp.)	
Calories	113
Carbohydrates	2g
Total Sugars	0g
Fiber	0g
Fat	10g
Cholesterol	33mg
Sodium	172mg
Protein	4g

Stir stevia and milk in a small bowl until stevia dissolves and is mixed thoroughly. Add this to cream cheese in a larger bowl and mix ingredients with hand mixer until smooth and fluffy. Spread immediately on pumpkin bars or other dessert. Will keep in fridge for 3 days in airtight container.

*You can substitute regular cream cheese, but I prefer Neufchâtel cream cheese because it offers virtually the same flavor with less calories and fat.

Lisa's Note: For the same size serving (2 Tbsp.), one of the leading store-bought brands of cream cheese icing with sugar has 150 calories, 24 grams of carbohydrates (22 are sugar), 6 grams of fat and no protein. The other major drawbacks to the store-bought icings are the ingredients in most: of course sugar is the first ingredient, but then there's partially hydrogenated soybean oil, cottonseed oil, food dyes, artificial flavor and preservatives.

It's so easy to make the icing at home with low-fat cream cheese and stevia and so much healthier! The nutritional facts speak for themselves!

Versatile Vanilla Icing

Makes enough to spread on a large pound cake or one layer cake.

3 Tbsp. 2% milk
½ tsp. stevia extract (see page xii for brand variances)
1 ½ Tbsp. vanilla extract
1 ½ pkgs. (12 oz.) Neufchâtel cream cheese, softened

Stir milk, stevia and vanilla in a small bowl until stevia dissolves and is mixed thoroughly. Add this to cream cheese in a larger bowl and mix ingredients with hand mixer until smooth and fluffy. Spread immediately on cakes or other dessert. Will keep in fridge for 3 days in airtight container.

Nutrition Facts/Serving	
(2 Tbsp.)	
Calories	120
Carbohydrates	2g
Total Sugars	less than 1g
Fiber	0g
Fat	10g
Cholesterol	33mg
Sodium	173mg
Protein	4g

Chocolate Icing

Makes enough to spread on a pound cake or one layer cake.

4 Tbsp. 2% milk
¾ tsp. stevia extract (see page xii for brand variances)
4 Tbsp. cocoa powder
1 ½ pkgs. (12 oz.) Neufchâtel cream cheese, softened

Stir milk and stevia in a small bowl until stevia dissolves and is mixed thoroughly. Add cocoa powder and stir until well blended. Add this to cream cheese in a larger bowl and mix together with hand mixer until smooth and fluffy. Spread immediately on cakes or other dessert. Will keep in fridge for 3 days in airtight container.

Nutrition Facts/Serving	
(2 Tbsp.)	
Calories	120
Carbohydrates	3g
Total Sugars	less than 1g
Fiber	less than 1g
Fat	11g
Cholesterol	33mg
Sodium	174mg
Protein	5g

Sugar Comparison: *One of the leading store-bought brands of chocolate icing has 140 calories, 22 grams of carbohydrates (19 are sugar), 5 grams of fat and no protein.*

Variation: Chocolate Icing with Unsweetened Chocolate
Makes enough to spread on a pound cake or one layer cake.

3 Tbsp. 2% milk
1 tsp. stevia extract (see page xii for brand variances)
1 oz. unsweetened baking chocolate bar
1 ½ pkgs. (12 oz.) Neufchâtel cream cheese, softened

Nutrition Facts/Serving	
(2 Tbsp.)	
Calories	100
Carbohydrates	2g
Total Sugars	1g
Fiber	0g
Fat	9g
Cholesterol	25mg
Sodium	132mg
Protein	4g

Stir milk and stevia in a small bowl until stevia dissolves and is mixed thoroughly. Break chocolate bar into small pieces and melt for 30 seconds on high in microwave. Stir and heat another 20 to 30 seconds. Stir until chocolate is completely melted. Add milk and stevia mixture to chocolate and stir until well blended. Heat an additional 20 seconds. Stir until thoroughly mixed. Mix cream cheese with wire whisk of electric mixer. Then add chocolate and milk mixture to cream cheese and mix with hand mixer until smooth and fluffy.

Suggestions When Baking Cookies:

1. *Use parchment paper on cookie sheets instead of greasing them. This offers two main advantages:*
   a. easier cleanup
   b. lower calories and fat because of no additional oil/spray

2. *Use unsweetened dried fruit like coconut and cranberries. It is harder to find, but resources are provided if you need them. Again, save on extra calories and sugar content when you can!*

3. *Add some unusual extracts, such as hazelnut and cherry, to accent the flavors in the cookies. These are optional but can make a difference that's worth it.*

4. *As in the cakes, use unbleached flour and sea salt as these more natural ingredients are more nutritious and less refined.*

5. *As in the cakes, use unsalted butter because you can include the exact amount of salt you want in a recipe without the extra sodium you may not need in the salted butter.*

6. *As in the cakes, when mixing the butter with the eggs and stevia, be aware that the mixture will not "cream" as it does in traditional sugar recipes, rather the butter will still be separate from the eggs. But the mixture will incorporate when dry ingredients are added.*

7. *As in the cakes, place baking pans on rack in the center of the oven.*

Wonderful White Chocolate Chip-Cherry Cookies

Serving Size: 2 cookies • **Total Servings:** 13 (26 cookies)

2 large eggs
¾ tsp. stevia extract (see page xii for brand variances)
½ tsp. vanilla extract
¾ cup (1 ½ sticks) unsalted butter, softened

2 cups unbleached flour
¾ tsp. baking powder
½ tsp. sea salt
½ cup unsweetened dried cherries
½ cup white chocolate chips

Preheat oven to 350° F. Place parchment paper on two cookie sheets. Beat eggs, stevia and vanilla extract with electric mixer. Add butter and blend well until smooth and creamy. Sift flour, baking powder and salt, then add half to egg mixture. Mix well. Add the balance of the dry ingredients and mix thoroughly. Dough will be thick. Process dried cherries in food processor until in large bits. Fold chips and cherries into dough mixture.

Shape into 1 ¼" balls and press down with hand until about 2" flat onto baking sheets. Bake for 10 to 12 minutes or until bottom of cookie becomes slightly browned. Cool on wire racks.

Sugar Comparison

Nutrition Facts/Serving
-2 cookies

	This Recipe	Traditional "Sugar" Recipe
Calories	172	284- over 60% more!
Carbohydrates	17g	39g- More than double!
Total Sugars	6g	27g- 4.5 times more!
Fiber	less than 1g	less than 1g
Fat	10g	12g- 20% more!
Cholesterol	46mg	39mg
Sodium	90mg	124mg
Protein	3g	3g

Variation I: White Chocolate Chip-Cranberry Cookies

Replace cherries with dried cranberries. You can find great dried cranberries at Whole Foods Market or in the bulk foods section of some health food grocers. They cost more than most but are unsweetened, fresh and taste great!

Variation II: Chocolate Chip Cookies

Replace white chocolate chips for regular chocolate chips, increase stevia to 1 tsp. and reduce baking powder to ½ teaspoon.

Lisa's Note: *These cookies do not brown on top like cookies made with sugar, so first check the bottom of the cookies for browning. You can also put a toothpick in the center of one and see if it's dry. If so, then the cookie is done. The result will be a soft, cake-like "wonderful" cookie!*

Also, the dried cherries I used in this recipe are dried, pitted, tart Montmorency cherries from Kariba Farms. If you can't find this brand, try to get dried cherries with little or no added sugar.

White chocolate isn't really "chocolate" at all because it contains only the fat from the cocoa bean and other non-chocolate ingredients. So it's important to choose white chocolate chips or baking bars that contain only the cocoa butter as the "fat" ingredient. Avoid products that are all sugar, hard vegetable fat and have artificial chocolate flavoring. You see, the labeling rules for chocolate don't apply to white chocolate, so you need to read labels! Ghirardelli is one brand that has cocoa butter for a better chocolate flavor and contains less artificial ingredients.

Classic Coconut Macaroons

Serving Size: 2 (1 ½") cookies • **Total Servings:** 15 (30 cookies)

2 cups <u>**unsweetened**</u> *shredded coconut (or measure the equivalent of 2 ¼ to 2 ½ cups dried unprocessed,* <u>**long**</u> *coconut, see instructions below*)*
1 cup instant nonfat dry milk
½ cup + 2 Tbsp. boiling water
¾ tsp. stevia extract (see page xii for brand variances)
½ tsp. vanilla extract
¼ tsp. coconut extract (optional for even more coconut taste!)
4 Tbsp. unsalted butter

Nutrition Facts/Serving	
Calories	119
Carbohydrates	5g
Total Sugars	2g
Fiber	2g
Fat	10g
Cholesterol	9mg
Sodium	5mg
Protein	2g

If your dried coconut is in long strands, place one cup at a time in food processor until it is shredded in pieces about ¼" long. If it is already finely shredded, skip this step.

Add dry milk to coconut, stir and set aside. Mix boiling water with stevia until dissolved. Add vanilla, coconut extract and butter to water, stirring constantly, until butter melts. With an electric mixer or hand mixer, combine coconut blend and butter mixture and beat on medium speed. Cover mixture in large bowl and refrigerate for at least 1 hour or even overnight if you choose. When ready to bake, leave out for about 1 hour or simply microwave in microwave-safe bowl for 15 seconds. (This helps the butter become soft faster). Then, preheat oven to 325° F, place parchment paper on cookie sheets or spray sheets with canola oil spray.

With your hands, roll small pieces of dough into balls, about 1" in diameter. Arrange balls on cookie sheets. Bake for 15 minutes or until cookie bottom is lightly golden in color. Macaroons will be soft inside so be careful not to overbake. Cookies will enlarge when baking and will measure approximately 1 ½" in diameter when fully baked. Cool on wire rack.

Optional: When cooled, dip half of each macaroon in chocolate or carob sauce (see page 61). Place cookies on wax paper-lined cookie sheet and refrigerate until ready to serve.

*__*Lisa's Note:__ Finding unsweetened coconut may not be as easy as running to the nearest grocery store. I've found that most only sell the pre-sweetened type so you may need to look elsewhere. Here are some options if you can't find it in your local health food store.*

Good sources for unsweetened coconut as of March 2005:

1. *Low-Carb Connoisseur- (16 oz.)- $3.95, www.low-carb.com or call 1-888-339-2477.*

2. *ChefShop.com- (8 oz.)- $2.49, www.chefshop.com or call 1-877-337-2491.*

3. *Whole Foods brand (8 oz.)- $1.29, www.wholefoods.com for your nearest location. The stores also have other brands, including one that is organic.*

4. *Bob's Red Mill- (12 oz.)- $2.51, www.bobsredmill.com or call 1-800-349-2173.*

Lemon-Poppy Seed Cookies

Serving Size: 2 cookies • **Total Servings:** 16 (32 cookies)

2 large eggs
1 ¼ tsp. stevia extract (see page xii for brand variances)
1 tsp. lemon extract
¾ cup (1 ½ sticks) unsalted butter, softened
2 cups unbleached flour
¾ tsp. baking powder
½ tsp. sea salt
2 Tbsp. poppy seeds

Nutrition Facts/Serving	
Calories	154
Carbohydrates	12g
Total Sugars	less than 1g
Fiber	less than 1g
Fat	10g
Cholesterol	51mg
Sodium	94mg
Protein	3g

Preheat oven to 350° F. Beat eggs, stevia and lemon extract with electric mixer. Add butter and blend well. Sift remaining ingredients and add ½ to egg mixture. Mix well. Add the rest of the dry ingredients and mix thoroughly. Shape into 1 ¼" balls and place onto parchment-lined cookie sheets. Press balls down with hand until about ¼" thick and 2" round. Bake 12 minutes or until golden on bottom of cookie. Cool on wire racks.

Lisa's Note: *These cookies are a nice change from traditional chocolate chip or oatmeal raisin cookies, especially for lemon lovers! My son loves these...they remind him of his favorite muffins—lemon-poppy seed muffins!*

Chocolate Cherry Biscotti

Serving Size: 1 biscotti • **Total Servings:** 15

1 ¾ cup unbleached flour
¼ cup unsweetened cocoa powder
¾ tsp. baking powder
¼ tsp. sea salt

2 large eggs
2 large egg whites
1 ½ tsp. stevia extract (see page xii for brand variances)
½ tsp. vanilla extract
½ tsp. cherry extract (optional)
2 Tbsp. water
⅓ cup finely chopped dried tart cherries

Nutrition Facts/Serving	
Calories	101
Carbohydrates	19g
Total Sugars	4g
Fiber	1g
Fat	1g
Cholesterol	28mg
Sodium	69mg
Protein	4g

Preheat oven to 350° F. Combine first four ingredients in a large mixing bowl. Combine eggs, stevia, vanilla and cherry extract with a wire whisk in a small bowl. Add egg mixture to flour mixture stirring until well blended using the paddle of your mixer. (Ingredients will not incorporate thoroughly yet.) Gradually add water. Dough will be slightly wet but now incorporated.

Turn dough onto a flat, floured surface, add cherries and knead 5 to 6 times. You may have to add as much as 3 Tbsp. of flour as you knead. Dampen your hands to make it easier to work the dough. Shape into a 12" long log and place on parchment-lined cookie sheet. Flatten to about a ½ to ¾" thickness and about a 6" width.* Bake for 25 minutes. Remove and let cool for 10 minutes.† Reduce oven to 325° F. Slice biscotti and arrange on baking sheet. Bake 8 to 10 minutes and then flip biscotti and bake another 8 to 10 minutes.

*If you prefer smaller, more oval biscotti, make the log 12" long, 4" wide and 1" thick.

†If you prefer softer biscotti, do not bake again after slicing.

Lisa's Note: *Biscotti come in different forms. This biscotti is softer and chewier than others that are hard and break apart easily. Both, however, can be enjoyed dunked in coffee, espresso, cappuccino or tea. Also, keep in mind these biscotti are very slightly sweetened so you may want to add more stevia to suit your individual taste preference.*

Almond Biscotti

Serving Size: 1 large biscotti • **Total Servings:** 15

Based on my friend Rose Perri's recipe.

2 cups unbleached flour
½ cup slivered almonds
¾ tsp. baking powder
¼ tsp. sea salt

2 large eggs
2 large egg whites
1 tsp. stevia extract (see page xii for brand variances)
¼ tsp. vanilla extract
½ tsp. almond extract
¼ cup water

Nutrition Facts/Serving	
Calories	99
Carbohydrates	14g
Total Sugars	0g
Fiber	less than 1g
Fat	3g
Cholesterol	28mg
Sodium	61mg
Protein	4g

Preheat oven to 350° F. Combine first four ingredients in a large mixing bowl. Combine eggs, stevia, vanilla and almond with a wire whisk in a small bowl. Add egg mixture to flour mixture stirring until blended using the paddle of your mixer. (Ingredients will not incorporate thoroughly yet.) Gradually add water. Dough will be slightly wet but now incorporated.

Turn dough onto a flat, floured surface and knead 5 to 6 times. You may have to add as much as 3 Tbsp. of flour as you knead. Dampen your hands to make it easier to work the dough. Shape into a 12" long log and place on parchment-lined cookie sheet. Flatten to about a ½ to ¾" thickness and about a 6" width.*

Bake in oven for 30 minutes. Remove and let cool for 10 minutes.† Reduce oven to 325° F. Slice biscotti into ½" slices and arrange on baking sheet. Bake 8 to 10 minutes and then flip biscotti and bake another 8 to 10 minutes.

*If you prefer smaller, more oval biscotti, make the log 12" long, 4" wide and 1" thick.

†If you prefer a softer cookie, do not bake again after slicing the biscotti.

Variation : Anise Biscotti
Replace almonds with 1 ½ Tbsp. anise seeds and omit the almond extract.

Outrageous Oatmeal-Butterscotch Cookies

Serving Size: 2 cookies • **Total Servings:** 18 (36 cookies)

⅞ cup (1 ¾ sticks) unsalted butter, softened
½ tsp. stevia extract (see page xii for brand variances)
2 large eggs
1 large egg white
1 tsp. vanilla extract

1 ¼ cup unbleached flour
1 tsp. sea salt
1 tsp. baking soda
1 tsp. ground cinnamon
2 cups rolled oats
¾ cup butterscotch chips

Preheat oven to 375° F. Mix first five ingredients together in a bowl. Sift flour, salt, baking soda and cinnamon. Add this dry mixture to butter mixture and blend well. Stir in oats and chips. Place heaping teaspoonfuls onto parchment paper-lined cookie sheet and bake for 8 to 10 minutes until bottom of cookies are slightly brown.

Sugar Comparison

Nutrition Facts/Serving
-2 cookies

	This Recipe	Traditional "Sugar" Recipe
Calories	222	389- 43% more calories!
Carbohydrates	21g	52g- Almost 2.5 times more!
Total Sugars	7g	32g- Almost 5 times more!
Fiber	1g	2g
Fat	14g	18g
Cholesterol	49mg	51mg
Sodium	227mg	377mg- Almost 1.7 times more!
Protein	4g	4g

Variation: Oatmeal Raisin Cookies

Serving Size: 2 cookies • **Total Servings:** 20 (40 cookies)

Omit butterscotch chips and replace with raisins. Increase stevia to ¾ tsp.

Nutrition Facts/Serving	
Calories	179
Carbohydrates	20g
Total Sugars	6g
Fiber	2g
Fat	10g
Cholesterol	44mg
Sodium	196mg
Protein	3g

Pineapple-Pecan Cookies

Serving Size: 2 cookies • **Total Servings:** 17 (34 cookies)

2 cups unbleached flour
½ tsp. sea salt
¾ tsp. baking powder

2 large eggs
¾ tsp. stevia extract (see page xii for brand variances)
½ tsp. vanilla extract
1 cup (2 sticks) unsalted butter, softened
½ cup pecans, chopped into ¼" pieces
½ cup canned pineapple, unsweetened, in its own juice
  (drain juice and use only pineapple)

Nutrition Facts/Serving	
Calories	198
Carbohydrates	13g
Total Sugars	1g
Fiber	less than 1g
Fat	15g
Cholesterol	55mg
Sodium	89mg
Protein	3g

Preheat oven to 350° F. Sift flour, salt and baking powder in medium mixing bowl. In a large mixing bowl, beat egg, stevia and vanilla well with electric mixer or wooden spoon. Add butter gradually and continue to beat until creamy smooth.

Add dry ingredients to butter mixture, ½ cup at a time, stirring well with wooden spoon after each addition. Fold in the pecans and pineapple. Place parchment paper on cookie sheet. Roll tablespoons of batter into balls and place on sheet. Press balls firmly down with your hand to flatten. Bake for 15 to 16 minutes or when cookie bottoms are slightly browned. Cool on wire racks.

Lisa's Favorite Pies/Tarts

Keeper Key Lime – White Chocolate – Cheese Pie

Positively (Divine) Peanut Butter Pie

Sinfully Cinnamon Cream Cheese Pie

I selected my top 3 picks for the pies based on my preference and feedback from friends and family who tried the recipes. But I must tell you that the Rich Ricotta Cheese Pie is a very close fourth choice.

1. *I use Neufchâtel cream cheese in many recipes, including pie recipes, primarily because it has a third less fat than regular cream cheese and tastes great. Neufchâtel cheese originated in Normandy, France and is very similar to regular cream cheese, except that it uses whole milk, not cream. Frankly, I believe you sacrifice no loss of flavor with the lower fat cream cheese, but certainly a loss of calories and fat! You may, of course, substitute regular cream cheese if you desire.*

2. *Since many prepared piecrusts available in most local grocery stores have a few undesirable and unhealthy ingredients, I recommend using alternative all-natural brands for the times when you can't make your own piecrust. Whole Foods Markets and other large health food grocers carry some nice options, including Arrowhead Mills and possibly generic store brands. These all-natural piecrusts have better ingredients like expeller pressed soybean oil versus partially hydrogenated soybean or cottonseed oils. Another more desirable ingredient is organic evaporated cane juice versus corn syrup and high fructose corn syrup.*

All-American Apple Crumb Pie

Serving Size: 1 slice • **Total Servings:** 8

4 small Granny Smith apples
1 ½ tsp. ground cinnamon
1 Tbsp. unbleached flour
6 Tbsp. unsalted butter, melted
½ tsp. stevia extract (see page xii for brand variances)
1 chilled Particular Graham Cracker piecrust (see next
   page)*

Nutrition Facts/Serving	
Calories	350
Carbohydrates	31g
Total Sugars	7g
Fiber	5g
Fat	25g
Cholesterol	56mg
Sodium	95mg
Protein	4g

Preheat oven to 350° F. Peel and core apples and cut into ¼" slices.

Mix apples, cinnamon and flour in a medium bowl. Over medium heat, melt butter in a 12" frying pan. Add stevia and mix well. Add apple slices and raise heat to medium-high. Cook for 2 minutes covered. Uncover, stirring occasionally with large spoon and cook for 3 to 4 minutes more.

Gently place apples into chilled piecrust. Sprinkle crumb topping over apples and bake at 350° F until apples are tender, about 20 minutes. Serve with Whipped Cream Topping (see page 34). Pie is best served slightly chilled or at room temperature.

*If you don 't have the time to make your own piecrust, buy 2 pre-made graham cracker piecrusts. Use one for the main piecrust and ⅓ to ½ of the second piecrust for the crumb topping. Simply break the piecrust into small pieces and sprinkle on the top of the pie.

Lisa's Note: *While researching for this book, I found much discussion on the type of apple that is best for pies, but I think it's best determined by your personal preference. Nevertheless, here are some of the favorites mentioned: Arkansas Black, Baldwin, Empire, Golden Delicious, Granny Smith, Jonathan, Liberty, Northern Spy, Rome Beauty, Spartan and York. Source: www.allrecipes.com.*

Particular Graham Cracker Piecrust

Crust fits up to 9" pie.

8 Tbsp. (1 stick) unsalted butter, melted
⅛ tsp. stevia extract (see page xii for brand variances)
9 oz. graham crackers, (weight before crushed)*
2 Tbsp. raw wheat germ

Nutrition Facts/Serving	
Calories	251
Carbohydrates	26g
Total Sugars	4g
Fiber	4g
Fat	16g
Cholesterol	32mg
Sodium	93mg
Protein	4g

Melt butter in microwave for about 30 seconds. Add stevia to butter and stir until dissolved. Place half of crackers in food processor and process until crackers are in small pieces. Remove cracker pieces and place remaining half of the crackers in processor. Process until in small pieces. Place all cracker pieces in a large plastic storage bag and roll with rolling pin until finely crushed. Place cracker crumbs and wheat germ in a bowl and add butter. Stir with wooden spoon. Set aside ½ cup of crust mixture to use on top of crumb pie recipe. Press remaining crust mixture into a pie plate using the edge of a spoon. Fill or to pre-bake, bake in a preheated oven for 6 minutes at 350° F. Cool at room temperature, then refrigerate for one hour before filling.

*Lisa's Note: Health Valley Company (division of the Hain Celestial Group, Inc.) makes the healthiest graham crackers that I could find. I use the oat bran or amaranth ones for my crusts. Not only are they organic, but also they are low in fat, low in sodium, have no hydrogenated oils (almost impossible to find in a graham cracker) and taste great! Cane juice and unsulfured molasses do sweeten them slightly, but the actual sugar content is minimal compared to other graham crackers.

Wheat germ really tastes great in this crust. It adds a very interesting nutty taste, and is rich in vitamin E, vitamin B complex, protein, enzymes, minerals and more. I use it wherever possible to sneak it in my family's diet. Raw wheat germ is best!

Keeper Key Lime-White Chocolate-Cheese Pie

Serving Size: 1 slice •**Total Servings:** 8

4 Tbsp. key lime juice*
½ envelope unflavored gelatin
1 ¼ cups heavy cream
4 (1 oz.) squares Ghirardelli's white chocolate, chopped
12 oz. (1 ½ pkgs.) Neufchâtel cream cheese, softened
½ tsp. stevia extract (see page xii for brand variances)
½ - ¾ Tbsp. lime zest (optional)
1 prepared piecrust

Nutrition Facts/Serving	
Calories	610
Carbohydrates	42g
Total Sugars	11g
Fiber	5g
Fat	44g
Cholesterol	86mg
Sodium	546mg
Protein	14g

Pour lime juice into a bowl and gently toss gelatin in to soften. Heat ¼ cup of the heavy cream in a saucepan on low heat. Remove and stir in white chocolate until melted and liquid is smooth. Add lime juice mixture to chocolate and cool. Blend cream cheese, stevia and lime zest with electric mixer. Gently mix cooled white chocolate mixture into cream cheese mixture. Beat the rest of the heavy cream (1 cup) until it forms peaks. Fold this into white chocolate mixture then pour into piecrust.

Cover and refrigerate for 2 hours or until ready to serve. You may also freeze until ready to serve. Defrost in refrigerator for about 24 hours.

*Lisa's Note: You may be able to find a bottle of key lime juice at your local grocery store. But if you use Kermit's Key West Key Lime Juice for this recipe, you can reduce the amount of juice to 2 Tbsp. Kermit's Key West Key Lime Shoppe has locations in Florida and a Web site to order. For more information, call 1-800-376-0806 or go online to www.keylimeshop.com. They have a 16 oz. plastic bottle for $3.95. I've used this lime juice and it's fantastic! You can also email at Kermit@keylimeshop.com. Another key lime juice option is Nellie & Joe's Famous Key West Lime Juice – www.keylimejuice.com (for a local retailer nearest you) or call 1-800-lime-pie.

This is one of the most coveted pies by my family and friends at various social events. The cheese pie will really get rave reviews for you, too. However, since the nutritional facts are not as desirable as most of the other recipes in this book, I would reserve this pie for special occasions only!

Positively (Divine) Peanut Butter Pie

Serving Size: 1 slice • **Total Servings:** 8

1 cup (8 oz.) heavy cream*
¼ tsp. vanilla extract
¼ tsp. stevia extract (see page xii for brand variances)

4 oz. Neufchâtel cream cheese, softened
½ cup smooth natural peanut butter
¾ tsp. stevia extract (see page xii for brand variances)
1 prepared chocolate cookie piecrust (preferably Arrowhead Mills brand)

Nutrition Facts/Serving	
Calories	294
Carbohydrates	16g
Total Sugars	7g
Fiber	1g
Fat	23g
Cholesterol	31mg
Sodium	202mg
Protein	7g

Beat heavy cream, vanilla and stevia extract until stiff peaks form. Set aside.

Mix cream cheese and peanut butter in large mixing bowl. Using an electric mixer, beat at medium until well blended. Add ¾ tsp. stevia extract and whipped cream mixture to the peanut butter/cheese mixture. Beat until smooth. Place filling into piecrust and cover. Refrigerate or freeze for at least 2 hours. Prior to serving, if frozen, defrost on counter for about 30 minutes.

*1 cup heavy cream yields about 2 cups whipped cream.

Optional:

1. Make homemade piecrust (graham cracker, not chocolate) on page 23 if you have time or be sure to purchase one that has all-natural, healthy ingredients, not refined sugar or hydrogenated oils.

2. Decorate top of pie with another batch of whipped cream and add chocolate chips on top or drizzle with melted chocolate sauce (see page 61).

Lisa's Note: *I strongly recommend using all-natural peanut butter, as opposed to the highly commercialized peanut butters. The main reason is simply the ingredients. Some popular brands have the following added ingredients that are not necessary or healthy: sugar, partially hydrogenated vegetable oils (can include cottonseed, soybean and/or rapeseed), monoglycerides, diglycerides, salt and molasses. The natural peanut butters are simply raw or roasted peanuts and usually offer salted or unsalted versions.*

Chocolate Cream Pie

Serving Size: 1 slice • **Total Servings:** 8

⅓ cup cornstarch
2 Tbsp. unsweetened cocoa powder
1 ¾ cup 1% milk
1 ¼ tsp. stevia extract (see page xii for brand variances)
3 stevia packets (optional)
1 oz. unsweetened baking chocolate, chopped
1 large egg, beaten
1 tsp. vanilla extract
1 Tbsp. unsalted butter
prepared piecrust (preferably Arrowhead Mills brand
     chocolate cookie crust)

Sift cornstarch and cocoa powder into a bowl and then combine them in a small saucepan. Measure milk in measuring cup and thoroughly stir in stevia extract and packets; set aside. Place chocolate in microwave- safe bowl and melt for 30 to 40 seconds. Stir. Be sure not to burn, microwave in 5 to 10 second intervals after 30 seconds until thoroughly melted.

Slowly add milk/stevia mixture and melted chocolate to cornstarch/cocoa mixture in saucepan, stirring over medium heat. Stir constantly until thick. Add a small amount of mixture to beaten egg, stir, then put in the saucepan. Add vanilla and butter. Cook a few more minutes until very thick and then pour into a piecrust. Cover with plastic wrap to prevent skin from forming. Refrigerate for 2 hours and serve. This pie also freezes well.

Optional: When cooled, spread pie with Whipped Cream Topping (see page 34) and serve.

Lisa's Note: This recipe works without stevia packets, but I think they really add to the flavor.

This recipe originated from Karen Tripp, a recovered candida sufferer, who provides information on dealing with this condition on her Web site. Search the web under "Karen Tripp" for more information.

Sugar Comparison

Nutrition Facts/Serving
-1 slice

	This Recipe	Traditional "Sugar" Recipe
Calories	187	415- More than double!
Carbohydrates	22g	60g- 2.7 times more!
Total Sugars	9g	41g- 4.5 times more!
Fiber	1g	2g
Fat	11g	19g- More than 60% more!
Cholesterol	33mg	90mg- 2.7 times more!
Sodium	117mg	324mg- Almost 3 times more!
Protein	4g	7g

Rich Ricotta Cheese Pie

Serving Size: 1 slice • **Total Servings:** 8

¼ cup 2% milk
½ tsp. vanilla extract
1 ¼ tsp. stevia extract (see page xii for brand variances)
3 cups part-skim ricotta cheese
2 Tbsp. unbleached flour
3 large eggs
1 prepared piecrust

Nutrition Facts/Serving	
Calories	166
Carbohydrates	7g
Total Sugars	less than 1g
Fiber	0g
Fat	9g
Cholesterol	108mg
Sodium	145mg
Protein	13g

Preheat oven to 350° F. Measure milk in small bowl. Add vanilla and stevia extract. Stir until stevia is dissolved. In a large bowl, beat cheese, milk/stevia mixture and flour with mixer on high speed until blended. Add 3 eggs to mixture and then beat on low speed just until combined. Pour filling into a prepared piecrust. Bake for 40 minutes or until pie seems almost set when shaken. Cool in oven for at least 30 minutes after baking. Make sure to turn oven off and leave oven door open slightly. (Use a wooden spoon if you have one. This helps the cake have a gradual change in temperature from oven to your counter.) Chill cake in fridge for at least 4 hours before serving.

Variation: Pineapple-Ricotta Cheesecake

1. Double recipe above. Makes 16 servings.
2. Make Ricotta Cheese Cake Crust recipe (page 28) and pour cheese filling in spring form pan. Bake for 50 minutes. Cool in oven for a least 30 minutes. Remove from oven and cool additional 30 minutes. Remove sides of the spring form pan and cool completely. Spread Pineapple Topping evenly over cheesecake (see page 29). Refrigerate until ready to serve.

Lisa's Note: To avoid cracking of the cheesecake...

1. Make sure cake is firm around edges and center still "jiggles" a little when pan is shaken. It will completely set when cooled.

2. Don't overbeat the batter, especially after eggs have been added.

Ricotta Cheesecake Crust

Serving Size: 1 slice • **Total Servings:** 16

4 ½ Tbsp. unsalted butter, melted
pinch of stevia extract (see page xii for brand variances)
5 oz. graham crackers, (weight before crushed)*
1 Tbsp. raw wheat germ

Melt butter in microwave for about 30 seconds. Add stevia to butter and stir until stevia is dissolved. Place half of the crackers in food processor and make small pieces. Remove cracker pieces and place remaining half of crackers in processor. Process until in very small pieces. Place all cracker pieces in a large plastic storage bag and roll with rolling pin until finely crushed. Place cracker crumbs and wheat germ in a bowl and add the butter. Stir with wooden spoon. Using the edge of a spoon or your fingers, press crust mixture evenly into a 9 ¾" spring form pan.

*See page 23 for graham cracker suggestions.

Pineapple Topping

Serving Size: 1/16 • **Total Servings:** 16

2 (20 oz.) cans unsweetened, crushed pineapple (in its own juice)*
1/8 tsp. stevia extract (see page xii for brand variances)
1/2 Tbsp. lemon juice

Drain pineapple juice from crushed pieces. Add stevia and lemon to pineapple. Mix thoroughly. Spread evenly over cheesecake. Serve or refrigerate until ready to serve.

*Be sure the pineapple is in its own juice and has no added sugar!

†The stevia recipe includes pineapple topping, whereas the "sugar" recipe does not, so if you make a plain cheesecake, you'll reduce the carbohydrates and sugars even more!

Sugar Comparison

Nutrition Facts/Serving
-1 slice

If you made a standard recipe for this cake using sugar, whole milk ricotta, more eggs and heavy cream, the nutrition facts per serving would look like these per slice:

	This Recipe†	Traditional "Sugar" Recipe
Calories	277	355-Almost 30%more
Carbohydrates	24g	39g-Almost 1.5X more!
Total Sugars	12g	28g-More than double!
Fiber	less than 1g	less than 1g
Fat	14g	16g
Cholesterol	118mg	151mg
Sodium	205mg	177mg
Protein	14g	14g

Sinfully Cinnamon Cream Cheese Pie

Serving Size: 1 slice • **Total Servings:** 8

1 ½ cups heavy cream
¼ tsp. vanilla extract
¼ tsp. stevia extract (see page xii for brand variances)
½ cup 1% milk
¼ cup water
2 ½ tsp. ground cinnamon
1 envelope unflavored gelatin
1 (8 oz.) pkg. Neufchâtel cream cheese, softened for 1 to 2 hours
¾ tsp. stevia extract (see page xii for brand variances)
1 prepared piecrust

Beat the heavy cream for about 45 seconds using hand or electric mixer. Add vanilla and ¼ tsp. stevia extract and beat for about 20 seconds or until stiff peaks form. Set aside.

Mix milk, water and cinnamon in small saucepan and stir over very low heat for about 1 to 2 minutes. Remove from heat. Place gelatin in bowl and then pour milk mixture over gelatin. Stir until completely dissolved. Put through a strainer to remove any possible lumps from undissolved gelatin. Add this to cream cheese and beat in a large mixing bowl for about 2 minutes. Add ¾ tsp. stevia to cream cheese and beat again.

Fold in 1 cup of the whipped cream mixture until thoroughly blended. Spread mixture in piecrust. Spread the remaining whipped cream on top of pie. Place in refrigerator for about 2 hours before serving.

Lisa's Note: This pie can also be made using cinnamon chips. You can add 1 cup of the chips, delete the ground cinnamon, reduce the stevia to ½ tsp. and reduce milk to ¼ cup. You'll also have to increase the gelatin to 1 ½ envelopes. However, I prefer to use the other ingredients listed because they yield a delicious pie with fewer calories and sugar and are more natural.

Sugar Comparison

Nutrition Facts/Serving
-1 slice

*If you made this recipe the traditional way with cinnamon chips, regular whipped cream and sugar, here are the astounding statistics.

	This Recipe	Traditional Sugar Recipe*
Calories	281	612!- Over 2x as many!
Carbohydrates	14g	66g!- Almost 5X as many!
Total Sugars	less than 1g	56g!- Oh, my!
Fiber	less than 1g	less than 1g
Fat	23g	33g- Almost 1.5X as much!
Cholesterol	53mg	32mg
Sodium	253mg	369mg- Almost 1.5X as much!
Protein	6g	8g- 25% more

Banana Cream Pie

Serving Size: 1 slice • **Total Servings:** 8

2 large egg yolks
1 large egg
¾ tsp. stevia extract
1 cup 2% milk
3 ½ Tbsp. cornstarch
¼ tsp. sea salt
3 Tbsp. unsalted butter
1 ¼ tsp. vanilla extract
2 bananas, cut into small slices
1 Tbsp. lemon juice
1 baked whole-wheat piecrust

Nutrition Facts/Serving	
Calories	391
Carbohydrates	42g
Total Sugars	7g
Fiber	5g
Fat	22g
Cholesterol	92mg
Sodium	430mg
Protein	9g

Beat egg and egg yolks; set aside. Add stevia to milk and stir until stevia is dissolved; set aside. Mix cornstarch and salt in saucepan. Begin to heat on medium as you gradually add stevia/milk mixture, stirring constantly until thick. Be careful not to burn.

Take off heat when it begins to bubble. Add a little bit of this mixture to the beaten egg, then place egg with mixture back in the saucepan. Add butter and vanilla and stir. Chill in the fridge for 30 minutes, stirring occasionally.

A few minutes before you remove mixture from the fridge, slice bananas and coat with lemon juice in a small bowl. Place banana slices on the bottom of piecrust. Remove mixture from fridge. Pour filling over banana slices and into the pie shell. Refrigerate for 2 to 3 hours or until ready to serve.

Optional: Decorate top of pie with ½ cup of whipped cream before serving.

Lisa's Note: *Since bananas are high in carbohydrates and calories, this pie is also higher in carbs and calories, relative to other pie recipes in this book. However, this pie's nutrition facts would be more impressive when compared with a banana cream pie made with sugar. Keep in mind that the added sugar in a traditional banana cream pie recipe would increase the carbs and sugar content significantly.*

Peach Tarts

Serving Size: 1 tart (3 oz.) • **Total Servings:** 4 tarts

½ Tbsp. cornstarch
3 Tbsp. water
⅛ tsp. stevia extract (see page xii for brand variances)
12 oz. peaches, or 1 ½ cups, fresh or frozen, cut in
    small pieces and sliced thin
  If using fresh peaches, peel, remove stone and cut
    into ¼" slices.
  If using frozen peaches, defrost for 1 hour.*
4 tart shells (see instructions following this recipe)†

Nutrition Facts/Serving	
(Tarts with frozen store-bought shell)	
Calories	172
Carbohydrates	21g
Total Sugars	5g
Fiber	3g
Fat	9g
Cholesterol	0g
Sodium	105mg
Protein	3g

Preheat oven to 350° F. Dissolve cornstarch in water and mix. Add stevia and mix again. Place the peaches and cornstarch mixture in a small saucepan and heat over medium heat, stirring frequently, until the mixture thickens slightly and the milky color has disappeared. To check for thickness, place a small amount of peaches on spoon. If peach sauce very slowly drops back into pan and is not runny, then it is sufficiently thick. Remove from heat, fill tart shells, place on cookie sheet and bake for 15 minutes until peaches are bubbly and shell is slightly browned.

Optional: While baking, whip up 1 cup heavy cream with ¼ tsp. stevia extract and ¼ tsp. vanilla. Whip until stiff peaks form. When tarts are done, cool, and place a spoonful of whipped cream on top and serve immediately. You can also cover and refrigerate for 1 to 2 days.

*To expedite defrosting, place peaches in strainer under running water for a few minutes then gently dry them with paper towels.

†To use frozen pre-made tart shells, defrost according to box instructions. The frozen shells are mentioned only if you are in a hurry and can't make the homemade shells.

Particular Graham Cracker Tart Shells

Enough for 4 tart shells

---

4 Tbsp. unsalted butter, melted
4 ½ oz. graham crackers (weight before crushed)
1 Tbsp. raw wheat germ
pinch of stevia extract (see page xii for brand variances)

Melt butter in microwave for about 30 seconds. Add stevia to butter and stir until dissolved. Place crackers in food processor until crackers are in small pieces. Place cracker pieces in a large plastic storage bag and roll with rolling pin until finely crushed. Place cracker crumbs and wheat germ in a bowl and add butter. Stir with wooden spoon. Press crust mixture evenly into four individual piecrust containers using the edge of a spoon or the tips of your fingers. Fill individual piecrusts with peach mixture and bake.

Lisa's Note*: When comparing the nutritional facts of the frozen store-bought tart shells with the homemade shells, keep in mind the difference in the ingredients. One of the main ingredients in store-bought tart shells is partially hydrogenated vegetable shortening as opposed to unsalted butter in the homemade shells. While reducing butter intake is recommended, especially for those with heart conditions and high cholesterol, the potential dangers of partially hydrogenated oils is well known and many researchers suggest that everyone avoid these harmful ingredients. In addition, the store-bought shells have preservatives, while the homemade shells have the nutritional benefits of wheat germ, healthy graham crackers and no added sugar.*

For those on a low-carb diet, try just the peaches for a refreshing dessert!

Nutrition Facts/Serving	
(Tarts with homemade shell)	
Calories	285
Carbohydrates	35g
Total Sugars	9g
Fiber	5g
Fat	16g
Cholesterol	32g
Sodium	93mg
Protein	5g

Nutrition Facts/Serving	
(Plain Peaches Only)	
Calories	35
Carbohydrat es	9g
Total Sugars	5g
Fiber	1g
Fat	0g
Cholesterol	0g
Sodium	0mg
Protein	less than 1g

Whipped Cream Topping

Serving Size: 2 Tbsp. • **Total Servings:** 16

1 cup heavy cream
¼ tsp. stevia extract (see page xii for brand variances)
¼ tsp. vanilla extract

Whip the heavy cream for about 1 minute with electric or hand mixer. Add stevia extract and vanilla and beat until stiff peaks form. Serve immediately or place in refrigerator in airtight container—will keep for a few days.

Lisa's Note: Making this whipped cream is certainly not "rocket science" and some might say that a recipe isn't necessary. So consider this a convenience for those of you like me who want it just right.

Nutrition Facts/Serving	
Calories	52
Carbohydrates	0g
Total Sugars	0g
Fiber	0g
Fat	6g
Cholesterol	21mg
Sodium	6mg
Protein	0g

Sugar Comparison

You can't taste much, if any, difference between the store-bought whipped cream in the spray can versus the stevia whipped cream. From a carbohydrate/sugar standpoint, there isn't much difference, but from an ingredients' perspective, you might want to reconsider the store-bought. Consider these ingredients in some store-bought whipped creams - sugar, propellant, monoglycerides and diglycerides, corn syrup, mixed tocopherols (Vitamin E) to protect flavor, natural and artificial flavors, carrageenan, sorbitan monostearate and others.

Squares • Bars

Chocolate Brownies

Serving Size: 1 brownie • **Total Servings:** 12

⅔ cup unbleached flour
½ cup cocoa powder
½ tsp. baking powder
¼ tsp. sea salt

2 large egg whites
½ cup 2% milk
8 Tbsp. (1 stick) unsalted butter
2 large eggs
2 ¼ tsp. stevia extract (see page xii for brand variances)
1 tsp. vanilla extract

Preheat oven to 350° F. Spray an 8" square pan with canola oil cooking spray. Sift flour, cocoa powder, baking powder and salt. Beat egg whites until soft peaks form and set aside. Heat milk for about 20 seconds in microwave and set aside. In an electric mixer, beat butter, whole eggs, beaten egg whites, stevia extract, vanilla and milk in a bowl.* Then add dry ingredients to butter/egg mixture and mix well. Spread in an 8" square pan and bake at 350° F for about 15 minutes or until toothpick comes out clean.

Sugar Comparison

Nutrition Facts/Serving
-1 brownie

	This Recipe	Traditional "Sugar" Recipe
Calories	126	321- 2.5 times more!
Carbohydrates	8g	40g- 5 times more! WOW!
Total Sugars	less than 1g	28g- 28 times more! YIKES!
Fiber	1g	2g
Fat	10g	18g- Almost double!
Cholesterol	57mg	81mg- Almost 30% more!
Sodium	86mg	97mg
Protein	3g	4g

Options:

1. Add ⅓ cup chopped walnuts, raisins or even chocolate chips. Or, frost with chocolate icing (see pages 9-10).
2. Omit vanilla extract and replace with ½ tsp. peppermint extract.

Lisa's Note: *The butter/egg mixture will not cream as it does in traditional sugar recipes, rather the butter will be separate from the eggs. However, it will incorporate when dry ingredients are added.*

Carob Brownies

Serving Size: 1 brownie • Total Servings: 12

⅔ cup unbleached flour
¼ cup unsweetened carob powder
½ tsp. baking powder
¼ tsp. sea salt

8 Tbsp. (1 stick) unsalted butter, softened
2 large eggs
1 tsp. vanilla extract
2 tsp. stevia extract (see page xii for brand variances)
½ cup 1% milk
½ cup unsweetened carob chips
1 large egg white
⅓ cup chopped walnuts

Nutrition Facts/Serving	
Calories	163
Carbohydrates	12g
Total Sugars	5g
Fiber	2g
Fat	12g
Cholesterol	57mg
Sodium	106mg
Protein	4g

Preheat oven to 350° F. Sift flour, carob powder, baking powder and salt; set aside. Cut butter in small pieces, place in microwave-safe bowl and melt in microwave for about 30 seconds.

With an electric mixer, beat whole eggs and vanilla in a bowl. Add butter and stevia and mix again. Scrape bowl periodically at bottom and sides to assure thorough mixing. Heat milk in microwave for about 1 minute and add to butter mixture. Place chips in a microwave-safe bowl and melt for about 30 to 40 seconds in microwave, mix thoroughly, and add to egg mixture. Beat egg white to a soft peak and add to egg mixture. Then add sifted ingredients to butter/egg mixture and mix until smooth.* Spread in a greased 8" square pan. Add chopped walnuts on top pressing slightly into the dough. Bake for about 15 minutes or until toothpick comes out clean.

Optional: See variations as listed for chocolate brownies on page 37.

__Lisa's Note__: The butter/egg mixture will not cream as it does in traditional sugar recipes, rather the butter will be separate from the eggs. However, it will incorporate when dry ingredients are added.

These brownies are darker, more cake-like and richer than traditional chocolate brownies, but have all the health benefits of carob and none of the guilt from sugar or caffeine.

You can purchase unsweetened carob chips from Whole Foods Market. The brand they carry is Sunspire Unsweetened Carob Chips. They are all natural with no sugar added. You can also call for more information (510-686-0116).

I wanted to offer carob as an alternative to chocolate for a brownie recipe in an effort to expand your traditional options. Also, carob has valuable health benefits and some people may want to avoid chocolate due to caffeine and cholesterol content.

Carob, also called St. John's bread, algarroba, locust bean and locust pod is a good source of potassium, is slightly sweet and is fairly low in calories. The commercial "fake cocoa" is made from the pods of carob trees (the locust) growing along the Mediterranean Sea. You can purchase carob in different forms. I use the carob powder and unsweetened carob chips in this book.

Please try this low-fat, low-sodium, high-fiber and calcium-rich alternative to chocolate! You may actually love it! Some people can't even tell the difference between carob and chocolate. It's really very good and certainly worth trying! I was even surprised when my sons chose the carob brownie over the chocolate one in a side-by-side "blind" taste-test!

Pumpkin Bars

Serving Size: 1 bar • **Total Servings:** 12

8 Tbsp. (1 stick) unsalted butter, softened
2 large eggs
¾ tsp. stevia extract (see page xii for brand variances)
1 cup canned pumpkin
½ cup unsweetened applesauce

1 cup unbleached flour
1 tsp. baking powder
½ tsp. baking soda
½ tsp. sea salt
2 tsp. ground cinnamon
½ cup organic raisins

Nutrition Facts/Serving	
Calories	152
Carbohydrates	16g
Total Sugars	4g
Fiber	1g
Fat	9g
Cholesterol	57mg
Sodium	198mg
Protein	3g

Preheat oven to 350° F. Spray 11 x 7" glass baking pan with canola cooking spray.

With electric mixer at high speed, cream butter in large bowl for about one minute. Beat in eggs, stevia, pumpkin and applesauce. Blend the dry ingredients in a separate bowl, except for the raisins. Add this mixture to the pumpkin batter and mix well on medium speed. Fold in the raisins. Spread the batter in the baking pan and bake for 25 to 30 minutes. Bars are done when the top springs back after being touched. Cool in pan on wire rack.

Optional: Frost with cream cheese icing (see page 8). Omit raisins for exclusive pumpkin flavor and less natural sugar! Increase stevia to 1 tsp.

Lisa's Note: Keep in mind that the baking time is for a glass pan. If you are using an aluminum pan, reduce the baking time. Check at 15 minutes and continue baking until the top springs back when touched and toothpick inserted in bars comes out clean.

Sugar Comparison

For the same delicious taste, the only thing you sacrifice with this recipe versus the sugar version is the high carbohydrate content. Take a look.

This Recipe	Traditional Sugar Recipe
Sugar 4g	Sugar 18g
Carbs 16g	Carbs 25g!!!

Lisa's Favorite Crepes/Cobblers/Dumplings

*Delectable Dessert Crepes

These crepes are more time-consuming in the upfront preparation than the other desserts in this category, but if you make and freeze in bulk quantity, it's so simple to defrost in the fridge and reheat in the microwave for a really special treat whenever you want one. The other advantage to crepes is the ability for each family member or guest to choose his or her favorite topping that you may have available.

Crepes • Etc.

Delectable Dessert Crepes

Serving Size: 1 (8") crepe • **Total Servings:** 6

⅔ cup 1% milk
⅓ cup water
2 large eggs
3 Tbsp. unsalted butter, melted*
½ tsp. vanilla extract
⅛ tsp. stevia extract (see page xii for brand variances)
¾ cup unbleached flour
1 tsp. unsalted butter (for each crepe during frying)

Nutrition Facts/Serving	
Calories	147
Carbohydrates	13g
Total Sugars	2g
Fiber	0g
Fat	8g
Cholesterol	88mg
Sodium	38mg
Protein	5g

Replace butter with safflower or canola oil if you wish.

Place the ingredients in the order listed in a food processor or blender and blend at the highest speed for about 20 seconds. Remove any excess from sides with a rubber spatula and blend again for about 10 to 20 seconds. Cover with plastic wrap and refrigerate for one hour. This "rest" is vital for the gluten to mix properly in the flour.

Once it's "rested," get all of the necessary supplies handy: batter, crepe pan, melted butter, plate, waxed paper, long spatula and ladle.

Melt 1 ½ Tbsp. unsalted butter for use in coating the pan before cooking the first crepe. Keep butter next to crepe pan on counter for convenience.

Heat crepe pan on medium heat and cover the surface with about 1 tsp. or less of butter. Make sure to coat the bottom and up the sides evenly to avoid sticking. Use an extra long "mouthed" spatula if you have one. Remove from heat. Quickly pour and disperse in pan about ⅓ cup batter to help batter form an even thin layer. Be sure to move pan around on its sides to assure even coverage of batter. Cook for 1 ½ to 2 minutes. Turn crepe when edges appear cooked and start to pull away from pan, and bottom is lightly browned. Continue cooking crepe for about 1 minute or until small brown spots appear on the second side. Remove from pan and place crepe onto plate covered with waxed paper. Finish the batch placing the waxed paper between each crepe as you stack.

If serving immediately, fold crepes into quarters or halves and place on a plate. See optional toppings next.

Options:

1. Topping and filling possibilities for these crepes are virtually endless.
    - Try warm Chocolate Sauce (page 61), Carob Sauce (page 61), Sizzling Cinnamon Apple Slices (page 66), or Strawberry Yogurt (page 78).
    - Try fresh strawberries, blueberries, bananas, or nuts. Use your imagination!
2. To flavor the batter, add about 1 Tbsp. unsweetened carob powder or cocoa powder and increase stevia by one pinch.

Lisa's Note: *If saving for use within 4 days, cover crepes with plastic wrap and refrigerate for 3 to 4 days. If freezing, store in an airtight container for up to one month. I use the large freezer bags and defrost on the counter when I'm ready to use.*

Pear Cobbler

Serving Size: 1 piece • **Total Servings:** 8

Filling:
3 Tbsp. water
¼ tsp. stevia extract (see page xii for brand variances)
5 pears, cored, skin removed, sliced into 8 wedges
1 Tbsp. fresh lemon juice
3 Tbsp. water
2 Tbsp. cornstarch
2 Tbsp. vegetable glycerin (optional)

Flour mixture:
⅓ cup unbleached flour
⅔ cup oatmeal
¼ tsp. baking powder
1 Tbsp. ground cinnamon
4 Tbsp. unsalted butter
2 Tbsp. 1% milk
¼ tsp. stevia extract (see page xii for brand variances)
2 Tbsp. water
1 Tbsp. vegetable glycerin (optional)

Nutrition Facts/Serving	
Calories	183
Carbohydrates	30g
Total Sugars	12g
Fiber	5g
Fat	7g
Cholesterol	17mg
Sodium	12mg
Protein	2g

Preheat oven to 375° F. Spray an 8 x 8 x 2" baking pan with canola oil spray.

Filling:

Mix water with stevia in a large bowl until stevia dissolves. Add pears and lemon juice to stevia and water. Mix thoroughly in bowl and transfer to large frying pan. Cook for 10 minutes on medium high heat or until boiling. Lower heat, cover and simmer for another 5 minutes, stirring occasionally. Mix water and cornstarch separately and then add to filling. Add vegetable glycerin. Stir and cook until mixture is bubbling and has a thick consistency.

Topping:

Combine flour, oatmeal, baking powder and cinnamon. Cut in butter until mixture is in relatively large crumbs. Mix milk and stevia until stevia dissolves. Add milk, water and vegetable glycerin to flour mixture. Separate a third of topping mixture and mix in pear filling. Pour filling into baking pan. Spoon remaining flour mixture in clumps over pear filling. Bake 20 minutes or until top begins to brown.

Variation: Apple Cobbler

Replace pears with apples.

Lisa's Note: The vegetable glycerin adds a "syrupy" thickness to the cobbler mixture, so the consistency is more interesting. It's a good replacement for brown sugar in traditional cobbler recipes made with sugar. Derived from palm kernel oil, vegetable glycerin adds only about 26 calories per serving in this recipe. If you don't have it available, the cobbler still tastes delicious without it. You can order it from Frontier Natural Products Coop, www.frontiercoop.com or call 1-800-669-3275.

Blueberry Dumplings

Serving Size: 3 dumplings • **Total Servings:** 5 (15 dumplings)

---

1 cup self-rising flour
½ cup water
¾ tsp. stevia extract (see page xii for brand variances)
3 ½ cups canola oil (for frying)

Mix flour, water and stevia together. Heat oil on high in a 2-quart saucepan until a small piece of bread floats to the top when dropped in the oil. Reduce heat to medium-high. Drop 2 to 3 teaspoonful-size dough balls into oil and cook for about 2 to 3 minutes until slightly browned. Remove when cooked and drain dumplings on paper towel-lined plates. Continue process until dough is finished. Serve immediately with blueberry sauce (see recipe below) drizzled on top of dumplings.

Nutrition Facts/Serving	
Calories	197
Carbohydrates	25g
Total Sugars	4g
Fiber	2g
Fat	10g
Cholesterol	0mg
Sodium	319mg
Protein	3g

Blueberry Sauce

Serving Size: 2 Tbsp. • **Total Servings:** 5 (1 cup total)

---

1 ½ tsp. cornstarch
2 Tbsp. water
1 pinch stevia extract (see page xii for brand variances)
1 ½ cups fresh or frozen blueberries*

Dissolve cornstarch in water and mix. Add stevia and mix again. Place the berries and cornstarch mixture in a small saucepan and heat over medium heat, stirring frequently, until the mixture thickens slightly and the milky color has disappeared. Remove and top dumplings with sauce. If preparing in advance, cover in plastic container with lid and refrigerate. When ready to use, simply microwave for about 30 seconds until warm.

*For frozen berries, use one (10 oz.) package. This recipe will also work with other types of berries, fresh or frozen.

Nutrition Facts/Serving	
(Sauce only)	
Calories	27
Carbohydrates	6g
Total Sugars	4g
Fiber	1g
Fat	0g
Cholesterol	0mg
Sodium	less than 1mg
Protein	0g

Optional: Place a spoonful of Whipped Cream Topping on top (see page 34).

Lisa's Favorite Puddings/Mousses/Custards

Chocolate–Hazelnut Bread Pudding

White Chocolate Mousse with Raspberry Sauce

Choosing my favorites in this category was extremely difficult. Finally, I settled with the chocolate recipes. However, the other desserts that were a close third and fourth were crème brûlée and pumpkin custard.

According to the research I've compiled for this book, the differences between these three desserts are subject to interpretation and are often elusive. However, here's a brief, succinct outline to help clarify some of the confusion.

Pudding- a thick, soft dessert that contains milk, eggs, a sweetener (usually sugar), a flavoring and some thickener like flour or cornstarch. Pudding is prepared by steaming, boiling, baking and it even can be unbaked or uncooked, by chilling in the fridge until it sets.

Mousse- an uncooked and unbaked "pudding-like" dessert that contains whipped cream, egg whites, gelatin or a combination of these ingredients, along with fruit, chocolate, etc. It is chilled before serving. The word "mousse" is a French term meaning "foam" or "froth."

Custard- a thick, rich, creamy dessert made with eggs and/or egg yolks, cream or milk, a sweetener (usually sugar), salt, flavorings and often a starch. Custards are either stirred and cooked on the top of the stove or baked in the oven, then cooled or refrigerated.

Chocolate-Hazelnut Bread Pudding

Serving Size: 1 piece (approx. 2 x 3") • **Total Servings:** 15

---

3 ½ cups 2% milk
1 cup heavy cream
2 ½ tsp. stevia extract (see page xii for brand variances)
4 oz. unsweetened baking chocolate
4 large egg yolks
1 Tbsp. unsalted butter, melted
1 ½ tsp. vanilla extract
⅛ tsp. sea salt
1 cup chopped plain hazelnuts
1 large challah bread loaf, cut into ½" cubes

Nutrition Facts/Serving	
Calories	292
Carbohydrates	22g
Total Sugars	3g
Fiber	3g
Fat	20g
Cholesterol	99mg
Sodium	214mg
Protein	8g

Preheat oven to 350° F. Spray an 11 x 9 x 2" baking dish with canola cooking spray and set aside.

Combine milk and cream in a large saucepan (6 qt.). Simmer over low-medium heat and stir occasionally. Add stevia and chocolate and stir until melted. Cook until mixture comes to a low boil and remove from heat. In a small bowl, beat eggs yolks and slowly add ½ cup of milk/cream mixture. Whisk until mixed and then add remaining milk/cream until mixed thoroughly. Blend in butter, vanilla and salt. Fold in hazelnuts and challah bread. Place pudding into baking dish.

Soak pudding at room temperature or in refrigerator for one hour. Bake for 45 minutes, and if knife or toothpick inserted in center comes out clean, pudding is done. If not, check in another 3 to 5 minutes.

Optional: Serve plain or with Whipped Cream Topping (see page 34) or plain. It's pure decadence!

Variation:
    Instead of hazelnuts, try walnuts or almonds.

White Chocolate Mousse with Raspberry Sauce

Serving Size: ½ cup (4 oz.) • **Total Servings:** 4 (2 cups total)

¾ cup heavy cream
½ tsp. vanilla extract
¼ tsp. stevia extract (see page xii for brand variances)
1 (4 oz.) bar of baking white chocolate, chopped
⅓ cup plain low-fat yogurt

Nutrition Facts/Serving	
Calories	331
Carbohydrates	19g
Total Sugars	18g
Fiber	0g
Fat	26g
Cholesterol	68mg
Sodium	62mg
Protein	4g

Whip heavy cream in electric mixer for about 1 minute. Mix in vanilla and stevia extracts until stiff peaks form. Melt white chocolate in microwave at 50% power for about 1 ½ minutes. Stir white chocolate until completely dissolved. Add to half of cream/stevia mixture and blend. Refrigerate the white chocolate/cream mixture in one bowl and the remaining whipped cream in a separate bowl for about 15 minutes.

Remove bowls from fridge and add yogurt to remaining whipped cream and whip with electric mixer until stiff peaks form. Gently fold yogurt/cream mixture into white chocolate/cream mixture. Place in dessert cups or ramekins and refrigerate for 2 to 3 hours. Keep up to 2 days in refrigerator.

Optional: Drizzle with Raspberry Sauce. Excellent!

Raspberry Sauce

Serving Size: 1 Tbsp. • **Total Servings:** 20 (1 ¼ cups)

1 ½ cups fresh or frozen unsweetened raspberries, defrosted
⅛ tsp. stevia extract (see page xii for brand variances)
1 tsp. lemon juice

Nutrition Facts/Serving	
Calories	3
Carbohydrates	less than 1g
Total Sugars	less than 1g
Fiber	less than 1g
Fat	0g
Cholesterol	0mg
Sodium	0mg
Protein	0g

Thaw frozen berries for about 30 minutes. Puree or blend berries with stevia and lemon juice in food processor or blender. Add more sweetness based on your taste preference. Pour into container with lid and refrigerate until ready to serve.

Crème Brûlée

Serving Size: ½ cup (4 oz.) • **Total Servings**: 6 (3 cups)

½ cup heavy cream
2 large egg yolks
⅓ cup 2% milk
2 tsp. unbleached flour
8 oz. evaporated fat-free milk, canned
2 tsp. vanilla extract
⅓ tsp. stevia extract (see page xii for brand variances)
¼ cup (or 12 tsp.) fructose

Preheat oven to 350° F. Combine heavy cream and egg yolks in a small bowl and beat lightly. Set aside.

Stir 2% milk and flour in a heavy saucepan until smooth. Add evaporated milk to milk and flour mixture in the saucepan and cook over medium heat. Stir occasionally until mixture boils and then remove it from heat and cover.* While stirring, gradually add about ¼ cup of the milk and flour mixture into the egg and heavy cream mixture. Pour this mixture into the saucepan with the remaining milk and flour mixture and stir constantly until well blended. Stir in vanilla and stevia, and mix well.

Pour mixture evenly into six half-cup ramekins. Place ramekins in a large rectangular baking dish. Pour hot water into the pan about 1" inch from the top of the pan. Bake for 25 minutes or until custard is set. Remove ramekins from oven and pan to cool. Cover ramekins loosely with plastic wrap and refrigerate until completely cold.

Just before serving, place top broiler rack 2 to 3" from heat and preheat broiler. Add 2 tsp. fructose on top of custard in each ramekin. Broil on top oven rack for 2 minutes until slightly bubbly and browned. Enjoy!

*Be sure to cover to prevent a film from forming on the top.

Sugar Comparison

Nutrition Facts/Serving:
-1 ramekin

	This Recipe	Traditional "Sugar" Recipe
Calories	149	422- Almost 3 times as many!
Carbohydrates	15g	22g- Almost 1.5 times as many!
Total Sugars	9g	19g- More than double the sugar
Fiber	0g	0g
Fat	9g	35g- Almost 4 times the fat!
Cholesterol	98mg	383mg- Almost 4 times the amount!
Sodium	66mg	41mg
Protein	5g	5g

Lisa's Note: *I found that the best way to get some crunch to the topping of crème brûlée made with stevia was to use fructose, a terrific alternative to the traditional sucrose (or table sugar). Fructose in its pure form has a low glycemic index, like stevia. Pure fructose is NOT the same as high fructose corn syrup, which is a combination of 50% fructose and 50% glucose. High fructose corn syrup has about the same glycemic response as sucrose (or table sugar).*

For this recipe, I've purchased pure fructose by Estee products at my local grocery store. If you don't find it at your grocery store, check your health food store. Pure fructose creates virtually the same crunchy topping as regular sugar but doesn't have the negative glycemic response. Although fructose has these benefits, the caloric content is the same as regular sugar (i.e. 15 calories/tsp.)

If you're not sure about using fructose in your diet, check with your doctor.

For this recipe, chilled eggs are better to use than those at room temperature because they have firmer yolks and separate more easily.

Tropical Fruit Pudding

Serving Size: ½ cup (4 oz.) • **Total Servings:** 4 (2 cups)

1 cup silken tofu, chopped
1 medium banana
1 tsp. coconut extract (optional)
1 Tbsp. lemon juice
¼ tsp. stevia extract (see page xii for brand variances)
½ cup fresh or frozen strawberries
½ cup fresh or frozen mango, pureed

Nutrition Facts/Serving	
Calories	76
Carbohydrates	12g
Total Sugars	7g
Fiber	1g
Fat	2g
Cholesterol	0mg
Sodium	4mg
Protein	4g

Combine all ingredients in the blender in the order listed, except the mango. Blend until the consistency is creamy and smooth; set aside. Puree mango by itself in blender. Pour thin layer of tofu/fruit mixture into the bottom of single- serving dessert cups and then pour thin layer of mango puree. Alternate layers until cups are filled. Refrigerate for 2 to 3 hours. Will keep fresh for 2 to 3 days in the fridge.

Optional: Serve with Whipped Cream Topping (see page 34).

Pumpkin Custard

Serving Size: 1 large ramekin (4 oz.) • **Total Servings:** 8 (32 oz. or 4 cups)

¾ tsp. stevia extract (see page xii for brand variances)
1 ¼ cups evaporated fat-free milk, canned
¾ tsp. ground cinnamon
¼ tsp. sea salt
¼ tsp. ginger
3 large eggs
1 ¾ cup (15 oz.) canned pumpkin

Nutrition Facts/Serving	
Calories	79
Carbohydrates	9g
Total Sugars	7g
Fiber	2g
Fat	2g
Cholesterol	81mg
Sodium	148mg
Protein	6g

Preheat oven to 350° F. Lightly spray ramekins with canola oil cooking spray. Mix and dissolve stevia in evaporated milk and set aside. Combine dry spices in small bowl. With electric mixer, beat eggs and pumpkin into dry spices. Mix thoroughly. Gradually add stevia/milk mixture into egg/pumpkin mixture and stir until incorporated.

Pour into 8-4 oz. ramekins and place ramekins in a large casserole dish filled halfway with hot water. Bake for 25 minutes or until toothpick inserted in center comes out clean.* Let cool. Refrigerate.

*If you use smaller ramekins, such as 2 oz., reduce cooking time to 15 minutes and continue until 20 minutes if center is still wet.

Optional: Serve with Whipped Cream Topping (see page 34).

Strawberry Mousse

Serving Size: ½ cup (4 oz.) • **Total Servings:** 6 (3 cups)

1 cup fresh or frozen strawberries, defrosted
2 large egg yolks
½ tsp. stevia extract (see page xii for brand variances)
1 Tbsp. lemon juice
pinch of salt

½ cup heavy cream
⅛ tsp. stevia extract (see page xii for brand variances)
⅛ tsp. vanilla extract
2 large egg whites

Nutrition Facts/Serving	
Calories	101
Carbohydrates	3g
Total Sugars	1g
Fiber	less than 1g
Fat	9g
Cholesterol	96mg
Sodium	77mg
Protein	3g

Puree strawberries in food processor and set aside. Beat egg yolks in a saucepan. Whisk in stevia, lemon juice and salt. Cook over medium heat, stirring constantly, until mixture has thickened. Stir in strawberry puree and refrigerate until mixture is thick.

Whip heavy cream until soft peaks form. Add stevia and vanilla and whip until stiff peaks form. Beat egg whites until stiff peaks form and fold into whipped cream. Fold the whipped cream into the strawberry mix. Put in individual cups and refrigerate for a few hours.

Optional: Replace strawberries with your favorite fruit, such as raspberries, mashed bananas, mangoes or blueberries. Make double the whipped cream and reserve half of it for the top of the mousse. For added appeal, decorate with slices of strawberry or other fruit.

Luscious Lemon Cream

Serving Size: ½ cup (4 oz.) • **Total Servings:** 6 (3 cups)

---

1 ½ cups water
1 envelope unflavored gelatin
2 large eggs, beaten
½ cup lemon juice, approx. the juice of 2 ½ - 3 lemons
¼ tsp. stevia extract (see page xii for brand variances)

1 cup heavy cream
¼ tsp. stevia extract (see page xii for brand variances)
¼ tsp. vanilla extract
lemon peel strips (optional)

Nutrition Facts/Serving	
Calories	172
Carbohydrates	3g
Total Sugars	less than 1g
Fiber	0g
Fat	16g
Cholesterol	125mg
Sodium	42mg
Protein	4g

Pour water into saucepan and stir in gelatin. Cook on medium heat until gelatin is completely dissolved and bubbles. Remove about half of the gelatin/water mixture and mix with beaten eggs in a separate bowl. Pour mixture back into saucepan. Cook over low heat for about 2 minutes and stir frequently until slightly thickened. Remove from heat and place in a bowl. Stir in lemon juice and ¼ tsp. stevia. Chill in refrigerator for about 30 minutes, stirring occasionally until thick.

Whip one cup heavy cream for about one minute. Then add ¼ tsp. stevia and ¼ tsp. vanilla. Whip until soft peaks form. Fold most of the whipped cream into the lemon mix and save remaining whipped cream for topping. Place in individual cups and refrigerate for a few hours. For added appeal, decorate with lemon peel strips or fruit slices on top of whipped cream.

Lisa's Note: If you love fresh lemons and homemade pudding, you will truly enjoy this!

Rice Custard Pudding

Serving Size: 1 piece • **Total Servings:** 15

½ cup white rice
3 ½ cups 2% milk
3 large eggs
½ tsp. stevia extract (see page xii for brand variances)
2 Tbsp. unsalted butter, softened
1 ½ tsp. ground cinnamon, divided
2 tsp. vanilla extract
½ tsp. sea salt
½ cup organic raisins*
1 ½ cups hot water

Nutrition Facts/Serving	
Calories	98
Carbohydrates	12g
Total Sugars	6g
Fiber	0g
Fat	4g
Cholesterol	51mg
Sodium	120mg
Protein	4g

Preheat oven to 300° F. Cook rice according to directions on package. Combine rice and milk in a bowl. Set aside. Beat eggs in a separate medium bowl. Add stevia, butter, ½ tsp. cinnamon, vanilla, salt and raisins. Blend the rice and milk mixture with the egg mixture. Pour in a large casserole dish (9 x 11 ½"). Sprinkle ½ tsp. of cinnamon on top.

Place casserole dish in a separate baking pan (11 x 13 ½") and pour hot water in pan. Make sure that water fills to 1" from top of dish. Bake uncovered for 30 minutes and then stir. Sprinkle ½ tsp. cinnamon on top. Continue baking for 50 minutes. When a knife inserted in center of dish comes out clean, pudding is done. Cool and serve.

Lisa's Note: The best raisins I've found are Pavich Organic Raisins. They are large, plump, moist and delicious. They are worth the premium price! I've found them at Whole Foods Market. You can also buy them online by the case at www.pavichraisins.com.

Lisa's Favorite Specialty Desserts

Italian Cannoli

Chocolate-Covered Strawberries

Bananas Foster "Stevia" Style

Not only are these my favorite tasting desserts in this chapter, but they also are among the fastest and easiest to prepare! What a great combination!

Specialty Desserts

I especially loved creating these recipes because of their variety and novelty. Enjoy making the most basic applesauce to the quite unique and elegant Chilly Cherry Soup, Italian Cannoli or perhaps the Strawberries in Balsamic Vinegar! These specialty desserts are relatively easy to make, their presentation is very impressive and their taste is exquisite.

Italian Cannoli

Serving Size: 1 cannoli • **Total Servings:** 6

---

1 ½ cups part-skim ricotta cheese, drain water, if necessary
¼ tsp. stevia extract (see page xii for brand variances)
¼ tsp. vanilla extract
¼ tsp. ground cinnamon
2 Tbsp. dried fruit, as used in fruit cake (optional)
1 oz. mini chocolate chips or carob chips (optional)
6 cannoli shells

With electric mixer or by hand, blend ricotta cheese, stevia, vanilla and cinnamon thoroughly in a medium bowl.* Dice dried fruit in food processor and fold with chips in cheese filling. Refrigerate overnight or at least a few hours. Fill 6 regular-sized cannoli shells and serve immediately.

*Using an electric mixer produces a creamier filling.

Lisa's Note: I found two brands of delicious cannoli shells that you can buy to save yourself the extra work of making them. Ferrara and Bellino make wonderful cannoli shells that are available in many grocery stores. If you can't find them in stores, you can order them online at www.shopviviano.com. J. Viviano & Sons, Inc. Italian Importers also has a store in St. Louis, MO (314-771-5476).

Sugar Comparison

Nutrition Facts/Serving
- 1 cannoli (<u>with</u> chocolate chips and dried fruit)

	This Recipe	Traditional "Sugar" Recipe
Calories	178	259- Almost 1.5 times as many!
Carbohydrates	15g	31g- More than double!
Total Sugars	9g	26g- Almost 3 times as many!
Fiber	0g	less than 1g
Fat	10g	12g- 20% more fat
Cholesterol	19mg	29mg
Sodium	85mg	51mg
Protein	9g	8g

Variation: Plain Cannoli
(<u>without</u> chocolate chips or dried fruit)

Lisa's Note: *If you omit the chocolate chips and dried fruit, you will drastically reduce your carbohydrates from 15g to 5g and sugar from 9g to 1g! Wow! The plain cannoli are still outrageously good! For those who are on very strict low-carb diets, you can further reduce your carbs by cutting out the shell altogether and simply enjoying the filling!*

The stevia taste is best when filling is refrigerated overnight and served the next day. If you're in a hurry, serve refrigerated after a few hours for a similar effect.

Believe me...these cannoli are so good, you'll want to make them frequently. Not only are they delicious, but they are so easy to make and will be enjoyed by everyone. When I first developed the recipe, I was very apprehensive about presenting the cannoli to my Italian family. But I was thrilled when everyone— even my parents who were used to the finest cannoli from famous Italian bakeries of South Philadelphia—said they tasted great!

Nutrition Facts/Serving	
Calories	143
Carbohydrates	5g
Total Sugars	1g
Fiber	0g
Fat	10g
Cholesterol	31mg
Sodium	54mg
Protein	8g

Chilly Cherry Soup

Serving Size: 1 cup (8 oz.) • **Total Servings:** 4 (32 oz.)

3 cups (24 oz.) pitted, unsweetened, dark red cherries (fresh or frozen)*
½ cup Whipped Cream Topping (see page 34)
2 cups water
1 ½ Tbsp. unbleached flour
¼ cup balsamic vinegar
⅛ tsp. stevia extract (see page xii for brand variances)
½ tsp. ground cinnamon

Nutrition Facts/Serving	
Calories	189
Carbohydrates	31g
Total Sugars	29g
Fiber	4g
Fat	6g
Cholesterol	21g
Sodium	15mg
Protein	3g

If using fresh cherries:

Wash and dry cherries. Remove pits.

If using frozen cherries:

Thaw cherries for about 30 minutes. Drain over a bowl saving any juice.

Make Whipped Cream Topping and set aside.

Using a blender or food processor, puree the cherries while gradually adding water until the mixture is almost all liquid and only very small cherry chunks are apparent. Be sure to add only enough water to cherries to make 2 cups of cherry/water mix. Sift flour in small bowl to eliminate any small chunks.

Pour cherry liquid into a saucepan. Add flour, vinegar, stevia and cinnamon. Cook over high heat, stirring constantly, until mixture begins to boil. Reduce to medium heat until slightly thickened. Then, remove from heat and add the whipped cream. Stir thoroughly.

Place cherry soup in a bowl and refrigerate for 30 minutes to 1 hour. When ready to serve, pour into four soup bowls and add extra whipped cream on top with a sprig of mint or dash of cinnamon for garnish.

*I used frozen Montmorency cherries, which are very tasty! However, they are not available in all grocery stores. If you need a substitute, be sure the cherries are unsweetened.

Lisa's Note: *This cherry soup is so refreshing, especially in the summer...or whenever you wish for summer. Either way, you'll feel it with this sweet but tart, cold soup. The sugar content in this soup is high, relative to other recipes in this book, because of the natural sugar in the cherries. Use for special occasions.*

Carob Fondue/Sauce

Serving Size: 2 Tbsp.• **Total Servings**: approx. 8 (Makes about 1 cup sauce)

1 cup (8 oz.) unsweetened carob chips
¼ cup + 2 tsp. 2% milk
⅜ tsp. stevia extract (see page xii for brand variances)
¼ tsp. vanilla extract

In a 2-cup measuring cup, mix chips and milk. Microwave on high for 1 minute. Stir until chips are melted and mixture becomes smooth (you may have to microwave an additional 15 to 20 seconds). Stir in stevia and vanilla. If small clumps are still present, beat with electric or handheld mixer until completely smooth. Serve immediately over fruit, pound cake, angel food cake or your choice. Refrigerate leftovers and reheat in microwave.

Nutrition Facts/Serving	
(Carob Fondue/Sauce)	
Calories	104
Carbohydrates	12g
Total Sugars	10g
Fiber	3g
Fat	5g
Cholesterol	less than 1g
Sodium	75mg
Protein	3g

Nutrition Facts/Serving	
(Chocolate Fondue/Sauce)	
Calories	106
Carbohydrates	14g
Total Sugars	12g
Fiber	1g
Fat	7g
Cholesterol	less than 1g
Sodium	6mg
Protein	1g

Variation I: Chocolate Fondue/Sauce

Use chocolate chips instead of carob chips for true chocolate flavor. Reduce milk to ¼ cup only.

Variation II: Chocolate-Covered Strawberries

Use Variation I to make chocolate sauce. Dip strawberries and other fruit and nuts in the chocolate sauce and place on wax paper-lined cookie sheet. Refrigerate for 1 hour or more and enjoy. Delicious!

Lisa's Note: See page 38 for nutritional benefits of carob. Chocolate-covered strawberries are always a hit in my home! We also enjoy the sauce with raisins, walnuts and bananas! Use your imagination.

Strawberries in Balsamic Vinegar

Servings Size: ½ cup (4 oz.) • **Total Servings**: 4 (2 cups or 16 oz.)

1 pt. (16 oz.) fresh strawberries
2 tsp. balsamic vinegar
⅛ tsp. stevia extract (see page xii for brand variances)

Remove stems, rinse, drain and slice strawberries. Mix balsamic vinegar and stevia in a bowl. Gently stir in strawberries. Let stand for 5 minutes. Serve immediately.

Nutrition Facts/Serving	
Calories	29
Carbohydrates	7g
Total Sugars	7g
Fiber	3g
Fat	0g
Cholesterol	0mg
Sodium	1mg
Protein	less than 1g

Lisa's Note: *This simple, yet elegant dessert can be enjoyed by itself, with whipped cream or as a wonderful topping for pound cake, vanilla ice cream or frozen yogurt.*

You can purchase balsamic vinegar in grocery stores, kitchen specialty shops and even online. The prices range dramatically from a few dollars to almost $200.00. You can purchase some of the finest balsamic vinegar from Modena Italy at Williams–Sonoma. The least expensive, aged for 12 months, costs around $10.00 for 8.8 oz., while the most expensive, aged for 10 years, runs $42.00 for the same sized bottle. There are also many options available online that cost even more. So explore and experiment based on your culinary taste, palate and budget!

Bananas Foster "Stevia" Style

Serving Size: 1 banana • **Total Servings**: 2

2 Tbsp. unsalted butter
⅛ tsp. stevia extract (see page xii for brand variances)
¼ tsp. maple extract (or maple flavoring)
⅛ tsp. ground cinnamon
1 Tbsp. vegetable glycerin (optional)*
2 bananas

Nutrition Facts/Serving	
Calories	213
Carbohydrates	27g
Total Sugars	15g
Fiber	3g
Fat	13g
Cholesterol	32mg
Sodium	3mg
Protein	1g

In a medium frying pan, cook the butter and stevia over medium heat, stirring until the stevia dissolves, about one minute. Add maple extract, cinnamon and vegetable glycerin. Stir thoroughly. Peel bananas. Cut in half lengthwise, then in half horizontally.

Add bananas to skillet and continue to cook over medium heat for 1 to 2 minutes, turning to coat the bananas with the syrup, until they are softened but not mushy. Sauté until "syrup" gets slightly bubbly. Gently transfer bananas to ovenproof glassware and place in oven to broil for about 1 minute. Remove from oven and serve immediately.

*See page 44 for more information on vegetable glycerin.

Optional: Serve with nonfat or low-fat vanilla frozen yogurt, Chocolate or Carob Sauce (see page 61) or even Whipped Cream Topping (see page 34).

Blackberry Fondue

Serving Size: 2 Tbsp.• **Total Servings:** 8 (Makes about 1 cup fondue)

1 ½ cups fresh blackberries or 2 cups frozen berries,
   defrosted
1 pinch stevia extract (see page xii for brand variances)
1 ½ tsp. cornstarch
1 Tbsp. water

Nutrition Facts/Serving	
Calories	14
Carbohydrates	3g
Total Sugars	2g
Fiber	1g
Fat	0g
Cholesterol	0mg
Sodium	less than 1mg
Protein	0g

Puree the berries in blender or food processor for 45 seconds to one minute. Add stevia extract to pureed berries. Dissolve cornstarch in water. Place the pureed berries and cornstarch mixture in a small saucepan and heat over medium heat, stirring frequently, until the mixture thickens slightly. Remove and place in fondue pot. Keep warm over a burner.

Suggested items for dipping: pound cake, angel food cake, strawberries, apples, pears, melons and figs.

Lisa's Note: *Depending on your appetite for dessert, you may want to make more of this than the suggested serving size. Once you start dipping, it may be hard to stop!*

Fabulous Fruit Parfait

Serving Size: ½ cup (4 oz.) • **Total Servings**: 4 (2 cups)

---

1 cup heavy cream
½ tsp. stevia extract (see page xii for brand variances)
1 tsp. vanilla extract
1 cup fresh blueberries, washed*
1 cup fresh strawberries, washed, sliced*

Nutrition Facts/Serving	
Calories	240
Carbohydrates	9g
Total Sugars	6g
Fiber	2g
Fat	22g
Cholesterol	82mg
Sodium	24mg
Protein	2g

Whip heavy cream until soft peaks form. Add stevia extract and vanilla. Whip until stiff peaks form. Layer ½ of fruit in bottom of dessert cups and then ½ of the whipped cream. Repeat layers. Serve immediately or chill about 2 hours.

*Recipe may be made with any of your favorite fruits.

Sizzling Cinnamon Apple Slices

Serving Size: ⅔ of an apple • **Total Servings**: 6

4 large Granny Smith apples*
1 ½ tsp. ground cinnamon
6 Tbsp. unsalted butter
½ tsp. stevia extract (see page xii for brand variances)

Nutrition Facts/Serving	
Calories	163
Carbohydrates	14g
Total Sugars	12g
Fiber	2g
Fat	13g
Cholesterol	32mg
Sodium	2mg
Protein	0g

Peel and core apples. Cut into ¼" slices. Mix apples and cinnamon in a medium bowl. Over medium heat, melt butter in a 12" frying pan. Add stevia and mix well. Add apple slices and raise heat to medium-high. Cook for 2 minutes covered. Uncover, stirring occasionally with large spoon, and cook for 3 to 4 minutes more. Place apples on dessert plates and indulge. Serve immediately.

*For more apple choices, see page 22.

Optional: Serve with nonfat or low-fat frozen yogurt or prepared Whipped Cream Topping (see page 34).

Lisa's Note: *Keep in mind that the carbohydrate and sugar content of this dessert comes from the natural sugar in the apples!*

Applesauce

Serving Size: ½ cup (4 oz.) • **Total Servings:** 3 (1 ½ cups)

---

2 large apples
4 Tbsp. water
pinch of stevia extract (see page xii for brand variances)
⅛ tsp. ground cinnamon
1 Tbsp. wheat germ

Nutrition Facts/Serving	
Calories	63
Carbohydrates	15g
Total Sugars	13g
Fiber	2g
Fat	less than 1g
Cholesterol	0mg
Sodium	less than 1mg
Protein	less than 1g

Peel and core apples. Cut apples into small chunks. Place half of the apples and 2 Tbsp. of water in the processor and puree.* Scrape sides of processor for apple pieces that stick to the sides and puree again. Remove pureed apples from processor and pour into a bowl. Place the other half of the apples in the processor with the remaining 2 Tbsp. of water and puree. Add stevia, cinnamon and wheat germ and process again. Pour first half of pureed apples back into the processor and mix thoroughly. Puree until sauce reaches desired consistency. Serve immediately.

*Food processors that hold 3 cups or less cannot fit all of the apples at the same time, so you have to process the apples in two steps. But, if you have a larger food processor, the apples can be processed at the same time.

Lisa's Note: This applesauce tastes delicious without wheat germ, but if it's included it adds a slightly nutty taste that's full of nutrients, especially vitamin E.

Sugar Comparison

Take a look at the carb differences between two popular commercial applesauce brands versus this stevia recipe. The store-bought brands also contain high fructose corn syrup, corn syrup and/or water in addition to apples.

Carbohydrates- 22g and 27g versus 15g for stevia recipe
Of the carbs, 18g and 25g are sugar versus 12! That's 1.5 to 2 times the sugar!

Lisa's Other Favorite Desserts

*Wonderful White Chocolate Chip–Cherry Cookies

*Almond Biscotti

*Carob Brownies

*Strawberry Yogurt

*Chocolate–Cherry–Vanilla Truffles

*Chocolate–Peanut Butter Fudge I

*Frosty Espresso Frappe
–especially the way my husband makes it!

*Strawberry–Banana Shake

See pages xiv, 20, 40, 46 and 56 for more of my dessert favorites.

Positively (Divine) Peanut Butter Pie, page 25

Chocolate Layer Cake, page 4 with Versatile Vanilla Icing, page 9

Crepes

**Delectable Dessert Crepes, page 42 with
Sizzling Cinnamon Apple Slices, page 66**

Crème Brûlée, page 50

Crème Brûlée

Chilly Cherry Soup, page 60

Pumpkin Custard, page 52

White Chocolate Mousse Parfait with Raspberry Sauce, page 49

Sorbet•Mousse

Strawberry Mousse, page 53 and Mango Sorbet Cream, page 79

Double Chocolate Truffles, page 84
and Chocolate Cherry Vanilla Truffles, page 86

Maple Coffee Frost, page 94, Chocolate Cherry Biscotti, page 16 and Almond Biscotti, page 17

Biscotti•Coffee

Chilly Treats

Use the recipes in this section as a foundation to create your own refrigerated and frozen dessert masterpieces! Substitute the fruit choices with your favorite fruit! You're limited only by your imagination, so have fun!

Strawberry Yogurt

Serving Size: ½ cup (4 oz.) • **Total Servings**: 4 (2 cups)

⅓ cup fresh strawberries*
⅛ tsp stevia extract (see page xii for brand variances)
2 cups plain nonfat yogurt†
1 Tbsp. wheat germ

Blend strawberries in food processor or blender until almost liquefied. Mix in stevia. Place yogurt, fruit/stevia mixture and wheat germ in bowl and mix gently. Serve immediately or refrigerate. Yogurt lasts in fridge for about 2 days in plastic container with airtight lid.

*May use bananas, peaches or blueberries for variety.

†Substitute low-fat yogurt instead if it meets your dietary needs.

Sugar Comparison

Nutrition Facts/Serving

Take a look at how a popular store-bought yogurt for a _6 oz._ container compares with the homemade stevia serving of _4 oz._

	This Recipe	Popular Store-Bought Yogurt
Calories	72	160- More than double!
Carbohydrates	10g	30g- 3 times the carbs!
Total Sugars	10g	28g- Almost 3 times the sugar!
Fiber	0g	0g
Fat	0g	1.5g
Cholesterol	2mg	10mg- 5 times the cholesterol!
Sodium	94mg	125mg- Over 30% more!
Protein	7g	6g

Lisa's Note: Here are some hints when comparing commercial yogurt brands. **

- *Purchase those with "live, active cultures." Some companies extend the shelf life by pasteurizing their yogurts after the beneficial bacteria have been added. This actually kills the bacteria that provide many nutritional benefits.*

- *Make sure that Lactobacillus acidophilus bacterium (or L. acidophilus) has been added. Some do not have this, but it is a very important bacterial culture.*

- *Avoid those with artificial binders and stabilizers like Swiss or pudding-style yogurts.*

- *If you want pre-sweetened yogurt, read the label to check how it is sweetened. Look for those with honey or natural fruit juice as a sweetener and avoid sugar or artificial sweeteners. Unfortunately, as of the date of this writing, stevia can only be sold as a dietary supplement, and is not used in commercial yogurt.*

****The <u>Stonyfield Farm Yogurt Cookbook</u> by Meg Cadoux Hirshberg. Stonyfield Cultured Books, 1995.*

Raspberry "Sorbet" Cream

Serving Size: 3 oz. • **Total Servings**: 4 (1 ½ cups)

---

6 oz. unsweetened, frozen red raspberries, defrosted*
1 cup drained soft tofu, chopped†
¼ cup water
1 tsp. vanilla extract
⅛ tsp. stevia extract (see page xii for brand variances)

Nutrition Facts/Serving	
Calories	58
Carbohydrates	7g
Total Sugars	3g
Fiber	3g
Fat	2g
Cholesterol	0mg
Sodium	4mg
Protein	3g

Thoroughly puree defrosted berries in blender or food processor. Add tofu and water to berries and blend until mixture is smooth and creamy, about 1 to 2 minutes. Add vanilla and stevia. Mix thoroughly. Taste sorbet and add more stevia if desired. Serve immediately in dessert dishes or stemmed glasses.

*Use mango instead of raspberries for variety.

† For a thinner consistency, use silken tofu.

Lisa's Note: *Most of us already recognize many of the health benefits of tofu, but recently scientists have found another reason for us to add tofu to our diets…tofu has isoflavones that may lower your risk of developing cancer. Tofu also can reduce cholesterol, help kidney disease and may cause calcium to be better utilized to help keep osteoporosis away!*

Grape Gelatin

Serving Size: ½ cup (4 oz.) • **Total Servings:** 5 (2 ½ cups)

⅔ cup 100% grape juice, cold
1 envelope unflavored gelatin
1 ½ cups (12 oz.) 100% grape juice, heated to boiling
⅛ tsp. stevia extract (see page xii for brand variances)

Nutrition Facts/Serving	
Calories	70
Carbohydrates	16g
Total Sugars	14g
Fiber	0g
Fat	0g
Cholesterol	0mg
Sodium	6mg
Protein	2g

Place cold fruit juice in bowl. Add gelatin and stir. Let sit for one minute. Then add hot juice and stir until gelatin dissolves, about three minutes. Add in stevia and mix thoroughly. Pour into 5 single dessert cups or into a small glass container. Refrigerate for 2 hours and serve chilled. Get creative and try all kinds of juice—black cherry, white grape, apple.

Lisa's Note: *Santa Cruz, After the Fall and R.W. Knudsen are three brands of juice that are available with no added sugar or other sweeteners, just 100% fruit juice! Many of the so-called fruit "juices" on the market today contain high fructose corn syrup. Make sure you only buy those with no added sugar or high fructose corn syrup for your and your family's better health!*

Sugar Comparison

Compare the nutritional values of this gelatin recipe with the store-bought gelatin in cardboard packages that you mix with water.
Store-bought:
- Your sugar intake per serving is increased to 19g, a 26% increase!
- Your calories per serving are increased to 80, a 14% increase!

Other advantages to stevia grape gelatin:
It has *none* of the following:
- *No* added sugar, only the *natural* sugar in the all-natural fruit juice!
- *No* adipic acid or fumaric acid for tartness.
- *No* artificial flavor.
- *No* disodium phosphate and sodium citrate to control acidity.
- *No* Red 40 or Blue 1 dyes.

Frozen Strawberry Yogurt Pops

Serving Size: 1 popsicle • **Total Servings**: 5 (5 oz.) popsicles or 13 (2 oz.) popsicles

---

*2 cups unsweetened frozen whole strawberries, thawed
    slightly (or 1 cup pureed fresh fruit)
1 cup (8 oz.) plain nonfat yogurt
⅛ tsp. stevia extract (see page xii for brand variances)
1 tsp. vanilla extract*

Blend strawberries and a ½ cup of the yogurt in food processor until strawberries are finely chopped. Add remaining yogurt, stevia and vanilla. Blend until smooth. Divide mixture evenly among 5 plastic popsicle holders. Freeze for about 3 hours or until firm.

If you don't have plastic popsicle holders, you can divide the mixture evenly among 5 (5 oz.) paper cups. Cover tops of cups with foil, then make a slit in the center of the foil with a knife tip and insert a wooden popsicle stick into each cup. Freeze for 3 hours or until firm. Tear away paper and enjoy!

Optional: Use raspberries, bananas, blackberries or a combination of fruit!

Sugar Comparison

The main drawback to a store-bought popsicle <u>with yogurt</u> is the carbohydrate/sugar content. I didn't find many, but the couple I did find had 21g to 22g carbs and 15g to 16g of sugar. Of course, this is very different from these stevia popsicles that have only 4g to 9g of carbs and 3g to 7g of sugar.

Nutrition Facts/Serving:
(5 oz. popsicle)

Calories	51
Carbohydrates	9g
Total Sugars	7g
Fiber	1g
Fat	0g
Cholesterol	less than 1mg
Sodium	39mg
Protein	3g

Nutrition Facts/Serving:
(2 oz. popsicle)

Calories	19
Carbohydrates	4g
Total Sugars	3g
Fiber	0g
Fat	0g
Cholesterol	0mg
Sodium	15mg
Protein	1g

Berry Cream Ice

Serving Size: ½ cup (4 oz.) • **Total Servings:** 6 (3 cups)

---

1 cup fresh or frozen unsweetened berries, defrosted*
1 cup plain nonfat yogurt
¼ tsp. stevia extract (see page xii for brand variances)
1 tsp. vanilla extract
prepared Whipped Cream Topping (see page 34)

Nutrition Facts/Serving	
Calories	103
Carbohydrates	7g
Total Sugars	5g
Fiber	1g
Fat	7g
Cholesterol	28mg
Sodium	39mg
Protein	3g

Put berries and 3 Tbsp. yogurt in food processor or blender until crushed well. Combine remaining yogurt, stevia and vanilla in bowl and mix thoroughly. Add to berries and blend. Pour berry mixture into a large bowl. Fold in the whipped cream. Smoothen any lumps with more mixing. When smooth, pour into a freezer container and cover. Place in freezer for at least 4 hours before serving.

Since cream ice is very hard when frozen, let it sit at room temperature for about 20 to 30 minutes before serving.

*I used a combination of strawberries, blueberries and blackberries for this cream ice. You can use virtually any fruit you want for this, so get creative!

Lisa's Note: The consistency of the cream ice is different than you've probably had before, but nonetheless it's delicious. It's actually a nice combination of water ice and ice cream but more convenient because the recipe doesn't require the use of an ice cream maker.

I hope you're pleased that chocolate is a main ingredient in the confection recipes. If you're as passionate about chocolate as I am, you'll want to read this worthwhile information that encourages the use of chocolate in moderation, informs you of its benefits when chosen properly and reduces your guilt about ingesting it.

You may be pleasantly surprised to learn that certain types of chocolate have nutritional benefits. The benefits of unsweetened, unadulterated chocolate include the following:

- *Is a source of the antioxidants "phenolics" that are believed to lower the number of free radicals in your body that contribute to health problems, such as cancer and heart disease.*
- *Contains important trace minerals and nutrients including iron, calcium, potassium and vitamins A, B$_1$, C, D and E.*
- *Cocoa is also a leading natural souce of magnesium that helps the cardiovascular system and helps with hypertension problems.*

The key to getting the nutritional benefits of chocolate is to use unsweetened chocolate and cocoa powder, not the mass-produced "brand name" milk and white chocolate that contain far less chocolate solids and are high in sugar and other undesirable ingredients. Look for chocolate with the highest level of cocoa solids for the most nutrition.

Combining stevia with chocolate in these recipes may be the best way to satisfy the craving for "sweet" chocolate without the negative health consequences and caloric disadvantages of pre-sweetened chocolate confections.

Double Chocolate Truffles

Serving Size: 2 truffles • **Total Servings:** 15

---

1 Tbsp. 2% milk
1 tsp. stevia extract (see page xii for brand variances)
1 (8 oz.) pkg. Neufchâtel cream cheese, softened
4 Tbsp. cocoa powder
6 oz. unsweetened baking chocolate, finely chopped
¼ tsp. stevia extract (see page xii for brand variances)
cocoa powder, carob powder, coconut or chopped nuts in
small bowls for coating

Stir milk and stevia in a small bowl until stevia dissolves; set aside. Mix cream cheese with electric mixer. Add stevia/milk mixture to cream cheese and mix again. Sift cocoa powder and add to cream cheese mixture. Mix for about five minutes, scraping sides of bowl periodically for thorough mixing. Divide truffle mixture into two small bowls and place in freezer for at least 30 minutes to solidify cheese for easier handling.

Take out first bowl from freezer and form mixture into 1" balls using your fingers.* Lightly coat balls with a dusting of cocoa powder.† Place on cookie sheet lined with waxed paper. Remove second bowl from freezer and repeat process. Once all the mixture is formed into balls, freeze for at least 15 minutes so that truffles become more solid. Take out half of the truffles from freezer. Defrost at room temperature for 1 to 2 minutes only.

While truffles defrost, melt chocolate using a double boiler. Add stevia and mix thoroughly. Partially fill an ice cream scoop with the melted chocolate. Keep scoop in left hand above boiler and drop a truffle in the chocolate with right hand.** Gently roll truffle in scoop. When covered with a thin layer of chocolate, place truffle on spoon or fork and place against edge of scoop to remove excess.

Optional: Upon coating truffle with chocolate, you can either place on waxed paper-lined cookie sheet or immediately dip truffle in cocoa powder, coconut or your favorite chopped nuts.‡ Repeat the coating process with the other half of truffles in freezer. Refrigerate on waxed paper-lined cookie sheet until ready to serve and prior to freezing. You can freeze for about one month in a plastic container. Before serving, simply defrost at room temperature for about 5 to 10 minutes. These will melt in your mouth!

Instead of baking chocolate, use unsweetened carob chips. Then coat truffles with carob powder instead of cocoa powder.

*If you're like me and dislike the idea of getting sticky cream cheese on the palms of your hands and under your nails, you can purchase disposable "nursing" gloves that work great for this recipe. They're very tight to the skin so that you almost forget you have them on. Just make sure that you don't buy the rubber or latex cleaning gloves that have powder on the surface. The powder can get into the truffles and the gloves are often too loose for effective truffle rolling.

† This cocoa powder dusting is a must for dark chocolate lovers. It adds a more robust, rich Belgian chocolate flavor and consistency to the truffle coating. However, if you prefer a milk chocolate flavor, omit the powder and simply coat with the melted chocolate.

** If you're left-handed, keep scoop in right hand above boiler and drop the truffle in the chocolate with your left hand.

‡ My favorite nuts are macadamias, pistachios, hazelnuts, pecans and walnuts.

Sugar Comparison

Nutrition Facts/Serving
- 2 truffles

The nutrition facts of a traditional chocolate truffle recipe differ so much from the stevia version. The stevia truffles are better for your health, taste phenomenal and are easy to prepare... all these advantages without the guilt of truffles with sugar. The main ingredients in the traditional truffles are sugar, chocolate, heavy cream and butter.

	This Recipe	Traditional "Sugar" Recipe
Calories	103	445- Over 4 times more!
Carbohydrates	4g	39g- Almost 10 times more!
Total Sugars	less than 1g	34g- 34 times more!
Fiber	2g	5g- 2.5 times more!
Fat	10g	33g- Over 3 times more!
Cholesterol	12mg	38mg- Over 3 times more!
Sodium	65mg	8mg
Protein	4g	5g

Chocolate-Cherry-Vanilla Truffles*

Serving Size: 2 truffles • **Total Servings:** 15

½ Tbsp. 2% milk
1 tsp. stevia extract (see page xii for brand variances)
1 (8 oz.) pkg. Neufchâtel cream cheese, softened
1 tsp. cherry extract (optional)
1 Tbsp. vanilla extract
¼ cup unsweetened dried cherries, finely chopped
cocoa powder or carob powder for coating
6 oz. unsweetened baking chocolate, chopped
¼ tsp. stevia extract (see page xii for brand variances)

Nutrition Facts/Serving	
Calories	106
Carbohydrates	6g
Total Sugars	2g
Fiber	2g
Fat	10g
Cholesterol	12mg
Sodium	64mg
Protein	3g

Stir milk and stevia in a small bowl until stevia dissolves; set aside. Mix cream cheese with electric mixer. Add cherry and vanilla extracts and stevia/milk mixture to cream cheese and mix again. Fold in chopped cherries, scraping sides of bowl for thorough mixing. Divide truffle mixture into two small bowls and place in freezer for at least 30 minutes to solidify cheese for easier handling.

Take out first bowl from freezer and form mixture into 1" balls using your fingers. Lightly coat balls with a dusting of cocoa powder. Place on cookie sheet lined with waxed paper. Remove second bowl from freezer and repeat process. Once all the mixture is formed into balls, freeze for at least 15 minutes so truffles become more solid. Take out half of the truffles from freezer. Defrost at room temperature for 1 to 2 minutes only.

While truffles defrost, melt chocolate using a double boiler. Add stevia and mix thoroughly. Partially fill an ice cream scoop with the melted chocolate. Keep scoop in left hand above boiler and drop a truffle in the chocolate with right hand.† Gently roll truffle in scoop. When covered with thin layer of chocolate, place truffle on spoon or fork and place against edge of scoop to remove excess.

Upon coating truffle with chocolate, you can either place on waxed paper-lined cookie sheet or you can dust truffles again in cocoa powder for that extra chocolate punch. Repeat the coating process with the other half of truffles in freezer. Refrigerate on waxed paper-lined cookie sheet until ready to serve or before freezing. You can freeze the truffles for about one month in a plastic container. Before serving, simply defrost at room temperature for about 5 to 10 minutes. These will melt in your mouth!

*See Double Chocolate Truffles recipe for added tips and sugar recipe comparison, page 84-85.

† If you're left-handed, keep scoop in right hand above boiler and drop the truffle in the chocolate with your left hand.

Try any one of the following terrific recipe variations:

Variation I: Chocolate-Vanilla-Nut Truffles

Omit dried cherries and cherry extract and coat truffles with chopped nuts, such as pistachios, pecans, walnuts or hazelnuts.

Variation II: Chocolate-Vanilla-Coconut Truffles

Omit dried cherries and cherry extract and coat truffles with coconut after melted chocolate. Optional, for extra coconut flavor, add ½ tsp. coconut extract.

Variation III: Carob-Cherry-Vanilla Truffles

Use carob powder instead of cocoa powder and unsweetened carob chips in place of unsweetened chocolate.

Lisa's Note: If you do not include the cherry extract in this recipe, consider increasing the stevia extract by ⅛ tsp. Be careful of the dried cherries you choose. Some are loaded with added sugar, but if you look well, you will find some that have little or no added sugar besides what Mother Nature already put into them. Some brands, such as Kariba Farms, are available at health food stores. Whole Foods Market carries a few different options.

Chocolate-Peanut Butter Fudge I

Serving Size: 1 square (1 ½ x 1 ½") • **Total Servings:** 25

⅓ cup boiling water
¾ tsp. stevia extract (see page xii for brand variances)
4 Tbsp. unsalted butter, cut in small pieces
1 ½ tsp. vanilla extract, divided
1 cup (8 oz.) instant nonfat dry milk
1 pkg. (12 oz.) chocolate chips*
1 cup natural peanut butter†

Measure ⅓ cup boiling water and add stevia. Mix until dissolved. Add the butter and stir until most of it is melted. Add ½ tsp. vanilla extract and stir. Pour in a mixing bowl and add the dry milk. Mix until blended.

Place chocolate chips and peanut butter in a microwave-safe bowl and cover. Melt chocolate chips and peanut butter in microwave for a minimum of 2 minutes.** Stir well and microwave another 30 seconds or until the mixture is melted and smooth when stirred. Add butter/milk mixture to peanut butter/chocolate and blend well with electric mixer or by hand. Add remaining 1 tsp. vanilla and stir thoroughly.

Foil line an 8" square pan and place fudge in it. Flatten top with knife or wooden spoon. Cover and refrigerate for about 1 hour. Cut into squares. Keep refrigerated. Stays fresh for 3 to 4 days in fridge or in freezer in an airtight container for up to 2 months.

*You can use carob chips instead of chocolate chips.

† Before placing peanut butter in measuring cup, spray cup with vegetable/canola oil spray so it comes out easier and doesn't stick to the inside of the cup.

** You may need to melt the chocolate for as long as 2 minutes and 20 seconds. Watch carefully, you don't want it to burn!

Lisa's Note: If you use carob chips, reduce your microwave time by 30 seconds (1 min. 30 seconds first) and then microwave in 5 to 10 second increments if carob chips are not melted since they melt faster than chocolate chips.

Nutrition Facts/Serving (With Carob Chips)	
Calories	158
Carbohydrates	11g
Total Sugars	8g
Fiber	2g
Fat	10g
Cholesterol	6mg
Sodium	84mg
Protein	5g

Nutrition Facts/Serving (With Chocolate Chips)	
Calories	160
Carbohydrates	12g
Total Sugars	9g
Fiber	1g
Fat	11g
Cholesterol	6mg
Sodium	40mg
Protein	4g

Chocolate-Peanut Butter Fudge II

Serving Size: 1 square (1 ½ x 1 ½") • **Total Servings:** 25

⅓ cup boiling water
1 ¾ tsp. stevia extract (see page xii for brand variances)
6 Tbsp. unsalted butter, cut in small pieces
1 ½ tsp. vanilla extract, divided
1 cup (8 oz.) instant nonfat dry milk
6 oz. unsweetened baking chocolate, chopped
1 cup natural peanut butter*

Measure ⅓ cup boiling water and add stevia. Mix until dissolved. Add the butter and stir until most of it is melted. Add ½ tsp. vanilla extract and stir. Pour in mixing bowl and add the dry milk. Mix until blended.

Place chocolate and peanut butter in a microwave-safe bowl and cover. Melt chocolate and peanut butter in microwave for a minimum of 1 ½ minutes on high.† Stir well and microwave another 20 seconds or until the mixture is melted and smooth when stirred. Add butter/milk mixture to peanut butter/chocolate and stir well with electric mixer or by hand. Stir in remaining 1 tsp. vanilla extract.

Foil line an 8" square pan and pour fudge into it. Flatten top with knife or wooden spoon. Cover and refrigerate for about 1 hour. Cut into squares. Keep refrigerated. Stays fresh for about 3 to 4 days in fridge or in freezer in an airtight container for up to 2 months.

* Before placing peanut butter in measuring cup, spray cup with vegetable/canola oil spray so it comes out easier and doesn't stick to the inside of the cup.

† You may need to melt the chocolate for as long as 2 minutes. Watch carefully as you don't want it to burn!

Sugar Comparison

Nutrition Facts/Serving
- 1 piece

	This Recipe	Traditional "Sugar" Recipe	
Calories	138	109	
Carbohydrates	5g	20g- 4 times more!	The traditional "sugar" recipe contains sugar, evaporated milk, cocoa, peanut butter and butter.
Total Sugars	2g	19g- 9.5 times more!	
Fiber	2g	0g	
Fat	12g	3g	
Cholesterol	8mg	3mg	
Sodium	40mg	31mg	
Protein	4g	2g- Half the protein	

Lisa's Note: The Scharffen Berger dark chocolate adds a really rich taste to this delicious fudge. It is more costly than traditional unsweetened chocolate, but it's worth it! You can find it at some grocery stores, Whole Foods Market and other fine gourmet shops. If you want some special chocolate but don't want to pay for Scharffen Berger, use Ghirardelli unsweetened chocolate whose quality is also very good, but it is less expensive.

See page 25 for information about the benefits of using natural peanut butter.

Beverages

Use the recipes in this section as a foundation for you to create your own dessert beverage masterpieces! Mix and match your favorite flavorings in the coffee beverages. Try a combination of fruits and flavorings in the shakes. You're limited only by your imagination, so have fun!

Frosty Espresso Frappe

Serving Size: 12 fl. oz. • **Total Servings:** 2 (24 fl. oz.)

6 Tbsp. decaffeinated espresso coffee*
9 oz. water
⅛ tsp. stevia extract (see page xii for brand variances)
8 oz. ice cubes (about 5 ice cubes, enough to make 8 oz. crushed ice)
8 oz. nonfat milk
¼ tsp. ground cinnamon

Nutrition Facts/Serving	
Calories	79
Carbohydrates	13g
Total Sugars	6g
Fiber	0g
Fat	0g
Cholesterol	2mg
Sodium	59mg
Protein	6g

Drop espresso by the tablespoon in the basket filter of your espresso machine and add 9 oz. water. When brewed, add stevia to coffee and stir thoroughly. Refrigerate for 2 to 3 hours.† Crush ice in blender. Make sure to stop and start blender a few times to give the ice a chance to settle to the bottom before blending again. Stop when ice has a "snowy" consistency. Add chilled coffee, milk and cinnamon. Blend for about 15 seconds. Fill each large glass halfway and then fill both to the top to account for foam. Use spoon for occasional stirring since coffee will separate as you drink it.

Optional: Garnish with ground chocolate, cocoa powder, ground cinnamon, nutmeg or vanilla powder for added visual appeal and flavor. Enjoy with your favorite biscotti (see pages 16-17) or cannoli (see page 58-59).

Lisa's Note:

*If you don't like your coffee too strong, you could reduce the amount of espresso coffee called for in this recipe to 3 Tbsp. I've doubled the typical serving amount to make up for the dilution of coffee strength due to the addition of the ice and milk. If you're a purist, you can use regular coffee, but I prefer coffee without the stimulating effect of caffeine.

†If you don't have the time to refrigerate the coffee, the frappe will still taste great but won't be as chilled.

Sugar Comparison

When you compare coffee beverages from leading retail coffeehouses with the beverages listed in these recipes, you'll find the biggest drawbacks are carb, sugar and caloric content. For virtually the same ingredients as the stevia recipes (nonfat milk, coffee, etc.), but with the addition of sugar, comparable coffee beverages at the retail coffeehouses offer these ranges of nutritional facts: 24g to 34g carbs, 22g to 28g total sugars and 120 to 260 calories. This information is based on 12 fl. oz. with no additional ingredients.

Frosty Coffee Frappe

Serving Size: 12 fl. oz. • **Total Servings:** 2 (24 fl. oz.)

8 oz. freshly brewed decaffeinated coffee*
⅛ tsp. stevia extract (see page xii for brand variances)
8 oz. ice cubes (about 5 ice cubes, enough to make 8 oz.
    crushed ice)
8 oz. nonfat milk
¼ tsp. ground cinnamon

Nutrition Facts/Serving	
Calories	45
Carbohydrates	7g
Total Sugars	6g
Fiber	0g
Fat	0g
Cholesterol	2mg
Sodium	55mg
Protein	4g

Stir stevia in hot coffee until dissolved. Refrigerate coffee for 2 to 3 hours.† Crush ice in blender. Make sure to stop and start blender a few times to give the ice a chance to settle to the bottom before blending again. Stop when ice has a "snowy" consistency. Add coffee, ice, milk and cinnamon. Blend for about 15 seconds. Fill each large glass halfway and then fill both to the top to account for foam. Use spoon for occasional stirring since coffee will separate as you drink it.

Optional: Garnish with ground chocolate, cocoa powder, ground cinnamon, nutmeg or vanilla powder for added visual appeal and flavor. Enjoy with your favorite biscotti (see pages 16-17) or cannoli (see page 58-59).

Variation: Frosty Chocolate Frappe

Add ¼ tsp. vanilla extract and replace nonfat milk with nonfat or low-fat chocolate milk. This will add some carbs and calories due to the additional sugar in the chocolate milk.

Lisa's Note:

*This is optional, but you could add 1 ½ to 2 times the per serving amount of coffee you'd usually use in this recipe to make up for the dilution of coffee strength due to the addition of the ice and milk. For example, if you normally use 1 Tbsp. of coffee per 8 oz. cup, use 2 Tbsp. of coffee in this recipe. If you're a purist, you can use regular coffee but I prefer coffee without the stimulating effect of caffeine.

†If you don't have the time to refrigerate the coffee, the frappe will still taste great but won't be as chilled.

See page 92 for a coffee sugar comparison.

Maple Coffee Frost

Serving Size: 12 fl. oz. • **Total Servings:** 2 (24 fl. oz.)

---

16 oz. freshly brewed decaffeinated coffee*
⅛ tsp. stevia extract (see page xii for brand variances)
¼ tsp. maple extract
8 oz. ice cubes (about 5 ice cubes, enough to make 8 oz. crushed ice)
½ cup prepared Whipped Cream Topping (see page 34)

Nutrition Facts/Serving	
Calories	115
Carbohydrates	less than 1g
Total Sugars	0g
Fiber	0g
Fat	13g
Cholesterol	41mg
Sodium	15mg
Protein	less than 1g

Stir stevia in hot coffee until dissolved. Refrigerate coffee for 2 to 3 hours.† Remove coffee from fridge and stir in maple extract. Crush ice in blender. Make sure to stop and start blender a few times to give the ice a chance to settle to the bottom before blending again. Stop when ice has a "snowy" consistency. Add coffee and whipped cream. Blend for about 15 seconds. Fill each large glass halfway and then fill both to the top to account for foam. Use spoon for occasional stirring since coffee will separate as you drink it.

Optional: Garnish with ground chocolate, cocoa powder or vanilla powder for added visual appeal and flavor. Enjoy with your favorite biscotti (see pages 16-17) or cannoli (see page 58-59).

Lisa's Note:

*This is optional, but you could add 1 ½ to 2 times the per serving amount of coffee you'd usually use in this recipe to make up for the dilution of coffee strength due to the addition of the ice and cream. For example, if you normally use 1 Tbsp. of coffee per 8 oz. cup, use up to 4 Tbsp. of coffee in this recipe. If you're a purist, you can use regular coffee, but I prefer coffee without the stimulating effect of caffeine.

† If you don't have the time to refrigerate the coffee, the frappe will still taste great but won't be as chilled.

See page 92 for a coffee sugar comparison.

Chocolate Coffee Treat

Serving Size: 9 fl. oz. • **Total Servings:** 2 (18 fl. oz.)

8 oz. freshly brewed decaffeinated coffee*
¼ tsp. stevia extract (see page xii for brand variances)
½ tsp. almond extract
2 Tbsp. cocoa powder
½ cup prepared Whipped Cream Topping (see page 34)
8 oz. nonfat milk

Nutrition Facts/Serving	
Calories	163
Carbohydrates	10g
Total Sugars	6g
Fiber	2g
Fat	12g
Cholesterol	44mg
Sodium	66mg
Protein	6g

Pour brewed coffee into a bowl. Stir stevia, almond and cocoa powder into hot coffee. Add whipped cream to coffee mixture and stir until thoroughly blended. Pour milk into a microwave-safe container and heat on high power for 1 minute. Add milk to coffee/whipped cream mixture and stir. Pour liquid mixture into the blender. Blend for about 20 seconds. Pour into large glasses or mugs.

Optional: Garnish with ground chocolate, cocoa powder, ground cinnamon, nutmeg or vanilla powder for added visual appeal and flavor. Enjoy with your favorite biscotti (see pages 16-17) or cannoli (see page 58-59).

Lisa's Note:

*This is optional, but you could add 1 ½ times the per serving amount of coffee you'd usually use in this recipe to make up for the dilution of coffee strength due to the addition of the milk. For example, if you normally use 1 Tbsp. of coffee per 8 oz. cup, use 1 ½ Tbsp. of coffee in this recipe. If you're a purist, you can use regular coffee but I prefer coffee without the stimulating effect of caffeine.

The Chocolate Coffee Treat is the perfect compromise between hot chocolate and coffee. So if you can't choose between the two drinks or simply want a different taste sensation—have both with this delicious tasty dessert drink!

See page 92 for a coffee sugar comparison.

Strawberry-Banana Shake

Serving Size: 8 fl. oz. • **Total Servings**: 2 (16 fl. oz.)

8 oz. nonfat milk
pinch to ⅛ tsp. stevia extract
    (see page xii for brand variances)
3 Tbsp. silken or soft tofu
1 ripe banana
4 fresh or frozen strawberries
1 Tbsp. raw wheat germ

Nutrition Facts/Serving	
Calories	134
Carbohydrates	25g
Total Sugars	16g
Fiber	3g
Fat	1g
Cholesterol	2mg
Sodium	57mg
Protein	7g

Combine milk, stevia, tofu, fruit and wheat germ in blender and blend until smooth. Serve immediately in large glasses. For added visual appeal, place fresh strawberry on side of glass.

Variation I: Fruit Sensations Shake
Replace banana and strawberries with the following: blueberries, raspberries, mangoes and blackberries, or a combination thereof for a fruit shake taste sensation.

Variation II: Chocolate-Banana Shake
Replace strawberries with 1 Tbsp. cocoa powder and add ¹⁄₁₆ to ⅛ tsp. stevia extract.

Variation III: Fruit Yogurt Shake
Replace the tofu with low-fat or nonfat plain yogurt.

Lisa's Note: My family and I love these shakes, especially on the weekends for a quick, healthy, and delicious breakfast or for an afternoon pick-me-up! The ingredients are wholesome and healthy, and best of all, the shakes taste great! I use low-fat milk when I make the shakes for my sons. I recommend you use low-fat milk for older children and nonfat milk for adults. However, always check with your doctor about your specific dietary needs.

Ingredients Resource Guide

"All Things Key Lime"

Authentic Key Lime Juice, Cookies, Candy, Sauces, Marinades, Jelly, Pies, Pie bars, Cosmetics, Gift Baskets & Much More . . .

WE SHIP THE WORLD
1-800-376-0806
www.keylimeshop.com

"On The Hill"   *The aroma is free.*

JOHN VIVIANO & SONS
IMPORTERS OF ITALIAN FOODS WHOLESALE AND RETAIL

www.shopviviano.com
5139 Shaw Ave. St. Louis. MO 63110
1·314·771·5476

we put the dash in low-carb!

Low Carb Connoisseur

Call Toll Free: 888-339-2477
Online: www.low-carb.com

Reference Guide

Web sites:

www.allrecipes.com
www.baking911.com
www.bellaonline.com
www.bettycrocker.com
www.chefnorm.com
www.chefrick.com
www.chocolates-n-coffee.4t.com
www.cookierecipe.com
www.cookingwithstevia.com
www.cooks.com
www.cornsyrupnews.com
www.diabeticgourmet.com
www.doitwithdairy.com
www.dr-bravo.com
www.everydaycook.com
www.familytime.com
www.fatfree.com
www.flaxfood.com
www.foodhistory.com
www.foodnetwork.com
www.ghirardelli.com
www.gourmetsleuth.com
www.healthnotes.com
www.hungrymonster.com
www.joyofbaking.com
www.kitchenkapers.com
www.leaflady.org
www.mayoclinic.com
www.mountainroseherbs.com
www.newstarget.com
www.ochef.com
www.pastrywiz.com
www.raysahelian.com
www.recipegoldmine.com
www.recipestogo.com
www.romolochocolates.com
www.soyfoods.com

www.steviacanada.com
www.stonyfield.com
www.thatsmyhome.com
www.whatscookingamerica.net

Books:

Making Your Own Gourmet Coffee Drinks, Matthew Tekulsky
Pancakes from Morning to Midnight, Dorie Greenspan
Perfect Cakes, Nick Malgieri
The 5 in 10 Dessert Cookbook, Natalie Hartanov Haughton
The Frookie Cookie Cookbook, Randye Worth, M.A., R.D.
The Lady & Sons Just Desserts, Paula H. Deen
The Pancake Handbook, Siegelman/Conley/Kroening
The Soy Dessert and Baking Book, Brita Housez
The Stonyfield Farm Yogurt Cookbook, Meg Cadoux Hirshberg
Unbelievable Desserts with Splenda, Elizabeth Alston

Other:
Scharffen Berger Chocolate packaging insert

United States Dept. of Agriculture, Food and Nutrition Service, "Guidelines for the Amounts and Use of Nonfat Dry Milk, Whole Dry Milk, and Canned Evaporated Milk Which are Equivalent to One-Half Pint of Fluid Whole Milk," 3/22/72

Index

About the Author:

Lisa Jobs operated her own stevia business, @Stevia LLC, for almost nine years. During that time, she created many recipes using her own stevia products. With the help of her husband Chuck and two sons, Christian and Alex, Lisa perfected these recipes to bring you Sensational Stevia Desserts. Prior to owning her own business and having children, Lisa was in broadcast sales for major radio and television stations in the Philadelphia market.

She hopes that this book will help those who desire a healthier lifestyle, and those who need to reduce their sugar intake due to diabetes, obesity, or candidiasis. This book can also be a refreshing alternative for those who've tried recipes using chemical substitutes but either didn't like the taste or have experienced undesirable side effects! These delicious desserts using the all-natural sweet alternative, stevia, can help make a difference!

Lisa enjoys free time with her family and friends, reading about natural health, baking and cooking, scrapbooking, traveling and exercising.

To order additional copies of
Sensational Stevia Desserts,
call 1-888-8STEVIA (1-888-878-3842)
or go to www.steviadessert.com
For multiple copies, call 1-610-265-7102